No Place like Home

FRANK ALLAUN

No Place like Home

Britain's Housing Tragedy
(from the Victims' View)
and How to Overcome It

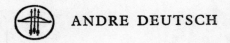 ANDRE DEUTSCH

First published 1972 by
André Deutsch Limited
105 Great Russell Street London WC1

Copyright © 1972 Frank Allaun
All rights reserved

Printed in Great Britain by
Ebenezer Baylis and Son Ltd
The Trinity Press Worcester and London

ISBN 0 233 95851 7: Casebound Edition

ISBN 0 233 96415 0: Paperback Edition

To Ruth

Contents

Acknowledgments

I offer my warmest thanks to all those whose help has made this book possible:

The men and women who were prepared to talk so frankly about their intimate and often embarrassing problems, sometimes at considerable personal inconvenience and at the cost of interference with their family duties.

The councillors and others who acted as 'leg men' to take me round the towns they know so well, to show me the good and the bad and to introduce me to residents with something valuable to say. Particularly Jimmy Wray and Mrs Bunty Urquhart of Glasgow; Jerry Malone and Hugh Dalton of Liverpool; Mrs Lois Fox of Paddington; Sir Robert Thomas, Ken Eastham and Joe Dean of Manchester; Sid Turner, Les Hough and George Stonehouse of Salford; and Joan Maynard, Vice-President of the Agricultural Workers' Union.

The indefatigible Mike Cantor of the research department at Transport House; the research staff in the House of Commons library; leaders of numerous tenants' associations, including Major Sam Waldman, Dudley Savill and John Evans; members of Shelter; Michael Goodger of Salford University; and senior officials of a number of local authorities.

The Members of Parliament who smoothed the way for me in their constituencies, particularly Neil Carmichael, Hugh Brown, Frank McElhone, Arthur Latham, Bill Stallard, Stan Orme and Eric Heffer.

The Guardian, Times, Daily Telegraph, News of the World, Tribune, Environment, Labour Weekly, trade union journals, and other papers for letting me use articles and letters I had written in their columns as the basis for proposals put forward in the two final chapters.

My wife for her tolerance of a husband's frequent absence on housing business and of his spending days at the typewriter when he was at home, for her suggestions of how to make the book interesting, and for being everything a true wife can be.

1*

Foreword

This is a book in which people are speaking for themselves, describing their own living conditions in their own words. It is not so much about bad housing as actually *by* families with acute housing problems.

The aim of the book is to show the misery caused by bad housing in the midst of what some people imagine to be a welfare state; to show the change that takes place after rehousing, though often marred by serious mistakes; and to suggest ways of tackling the housing problem generally.

The first person accounts are not 'horror stories', drawing attention to a sensational case; unfortunately they could be repeated several millions times. There are nearly eleven million men, women and children going to bed tonight in a house without a bath, hot water system or inside lavatory. More than five million of them live in dwellings held to be unfit for human habitation. Not to mention all those with other housing problems, such as overcrowding, dampness or soaring rents.

Part One

How the British People live...

. . . in the North and Midlands

1. Industrial slums

HARRY EARBY · JOHN MURRAY · EILEEN ECKERSLEY

HARRY EARBY: *Toadstools in the parlour*

A long street of decaying houses built in the last century, two identical parallel rows. No baths, no hot water, no inside lavatories. Not a blade of grass or a leaf to be seen. Typical of several million homes in the old industrial towns of the North and Midlands. This is where Harry Earby lives with his wife and three children.

We're young, the wife and I. Marjorie is twenty-five, I'm twenty-five and we have three young children. George, he's five. Then there's Julian, he's four, and there's Marie. She's three and a half. When we first got married we moved into a one-room flat, for which we paid £3 15s or £4 rent every week. Anyway, the first sight of a child and we decided we had to get out of the one-room flat. So we had this opportunity of a house, which belongs to a relation, which naturally we jumped at at the time. I hadn't actually seen the house before but the idea of a house seemed to be the ideal thing, and the rent was cheaper. At first it seemed ideal. It had three bedrooms and three rooms downstairs.

We had the first child. Everything was fair. But then the second child came along and we found we were in need of a bathroom and that an indoor toilet would be a suitable thing, which we hadn't got in this house. Not being particularly wise or foreseeing in any manner, we realised that the house was in a decrepit state. There was a great deal of damp in every room. There's damp in the kiddies' room and a considerable amount of damp in our room, and in these rooms downstairs too. The first opening of my eyes was when the floor collapsed in the hallway. Majorie was having the first child. What really sickened us was we were forced to put up with it. Marjorie was in a bad way with the child and every night I had to literally lift her over the hole to get her upstairs. I realised this was a damn state of affairs altogether. That was one of the first things that set the rot in with us. It upset us both.

Unfortunately we have a landlord who's not too eager to get on with these repairs. The house has been a constant cause of upset. It's dilapidated. There's no two ways about it. There's nothing really a landlord could do about the place except demolish it and rebuild it. There's a constant demand for serious repairs. There was a terrible need for these repairs in the front room. About three years ago the floorboards in there just gave way. Rotton. Pure damp right the way through. The first thing we noticed was that the sideboard was leaning on one side. I thought this was odd, and I stepped into this gigantic hole and just disappeared. I whipped the carpet back and the lino, and lo and behold there was a filthy big hole there. I picked a piece of timber up and it just crumbled away in my hands.

This was the first discovery of the water. It was about a foot deep. It was centralized in the middle of the room – and stagnant. I plastered one wall and by accident I happened to drop some plaster in the water. The smell of it was atrocious. A repair I've just done was a few days ago. I've just shored the toilet up. I don't know if you noticed it when you went out but there's a piece of timber there, a strut across. Well it had fallen down. The whole thing was coming down, and I banged the timber in. I had to do it. I would have mentioned it to the landlord but I knew that by the time he had got round to it the flaming lot would have come down and one of the kiddies could easily have been killed. For the cistern must weigh about 25 lb and with the weight of the water it must be 50 lb altogether. So I shored that up. But it's leaking as it is. When you flush it there's a leak somewhere. I must look at that.

On the subject of the kiddies this is something we have not experienced before. But in winter when they have to perform in bad weather, with snow or ice, they are going to have to use this toilet. Up to now we have had to use the potty for them. Nightly when we prepare them for bed we have to take the potty upstairs, one for the two boys and one for the little girl. We have to provide toilet paper which we must rip and leave on the dressing table or the fireplace just in case they want to perform a toilet in the morning. As regards hygiene, for my money it's absolutely ridiculous, because in the morning they are going to pass water etcetera, and it's in the room, it's in the air. We have a tremendous amount of mice, and I wouldn't know if this would attract them or not. But it would be possible, I should imagine. I dare say in these old houses it's only to be expected, it's only natural. They are very old and accessible to mice. This is the sort of thing we have to do. It's forced upon us merely because we have no indoor toilet; we have to use an outdoor toilet.

On this subject of cleanliness again, as regards a bath. When it comes to bath-time it's a case of using one of two things, the sink or a small bowl, which is about 18 inches or 2 feet across. A tin bath is out because we've nowhere to put it, as the kitchen is too small. We couldn't really leave it in the yard because we have an abundance of cats. They're constantly patrolling the yard and – etcetera. So a bath is absolutely out. In point of fact the kiddies have never experienced a bath. Up till nine months ago my eldest boy, George, he's five, had never seen a bath in his life. He was at one of the wife's friends where he saw one, for the first time. Julian and Marie have never seen one in their lives. So they don't know what a bath looks like. Or what an indoor toilet looks like either. So when it comes to bath-time about the best thing we can do is to get this plastic bowl out, fill it with hot water, and then we stand George in it to start with and then it's a case of a good wash down from head to foot, take George out, dry him off, put him down. Then the same process again. Empty the bowl, fill it with hot water, bring it in, place Julian in it. Same process again. On the settee. Dry him off. Then the same process with Marie. Place her in. Head to toe. Occasionally, if it's not too cold we can wash them in the kitchen sink. It's a bit larger and a bit deeper.

When it comes to hair washing time, well, it's rather a performance, because as you know, when you're washing hair, there's water everywhere. With kiddies they're splashing about. We take a chair into the kitchen in front of the sink, stand them on it, pour water over their hair, lather it up and rinse it off. But there's always a danger. We have a tremendous amount of draught in here and they are in the nude as a rule. So it's a hurry. Get it done quick. Dry it as fast as you can. Get another one in, get it done before there's a draught on them. But this is the nearest experience they have of a bath – a wash down in a little bowl. There's not much more we can do for them.

The kitchen, as I said, is very small. We have a cooker, a fridge and a washing machine in it. But we couldn't possibly put anything else in there at all. As a matter of fact I've just finished replastering the whole of the kitchen.

I plastered the walls about a year ago and, though I say it myself, it was rather a good job. But now you can see the damp. It's just pouring through. It's bringing the paint off and you can get your fingernails into the plaster. It's soft with water. Nothing can be done about that, I think. Repointing wouldn't make a fat lot of difference. It's just plain decay and old age. You could never get on top of it. It's the same story through all these houses. Old age has just got the better of them.

The kiddies are good. But what can you do? I mean you have a backyard. All these houses have backyards. Beyond the backyard there is an entry which is invariably cluttered up with empty tins, old furniture, carpets, bedsteads, and even the occasional mattress, which I've often removed myself from my own back gate. Beyond that there's another row of houses. And this system just carries on endlessly, front and back. In the front we have a street, a cobbled street, and next door to us we have a garage which is very very busy. It really does a good trade. So when we come to letting the children out, immediately we open the front door, of course, they're out. They go mad. They are off into the fresh air and they want to play. The first words which come out of my wife's mouth and mine are: 'Be careful. Watch the traffic. Don't go away. There's a main road over there. Don't play in the entry. You know what it's like. It's filthy dirty. Keep away from the garage; there are cars flying around.' This is the kind of thing which I imagine would grind away at a child over the years. Though I'm no authority I should think this would have some mental effect and I think it restricts them a great deal. Also, I imagine, with all the constant nagging you have to do, they will, after a time, feel a sense of resentment as regards play. As you know a child's life is 99·9 per cent composed of play. It likes the freedom.

A child has a natural instinct for adventure and discovery. There's an entry opposite my front door which leads directly onto a main road and another major garage. So the little one, Marie, she's three and a half, sees this entry. It looks delicious. So down she goes, past old dustbins, broken bottles. She ventures a little further onto Broughton Lane, which is an absolute death-trap, with the traffic. We've constantly shouted at them, but all of them, including George, will still persist in wandering down onto the main road.

It's not his fault particularly, it's just a natural thing with them. They want to wander, they've got to discover. You can't stop it. All we can do is nag at them, say: 'Don't move away from the front door. Sit on the step.' And they look at us as if to say, 'What's the use of living?' Which you can only expect.

The damp in the front room was very bad, though I have replastered it since, to no avail, because the damp is slowly coming through again. In another six months it will be as bad. Two years ago, when you came round to visit, Mr Allaun, we had told the landlord that the bay was leaking. It's always leaking, this bay. It has bad foundations and the brickwork, the uprights have gone, they're finished. It started raining in. So we put a bowl under this little hole and we mentioned it to the landlord. 'Yes,' he said, 'I'll get it done.' Fair enough. So he had it done. But the damn thing was rotten and it just came through again. So we had it repaired again and it seemed all right.

Then one day there was a really bad downfall of rain and the water was literally running down the wall. Marjorie and I discussed what we were going to do. We decided the best thing was to get the Sanitary in, if only for the sake of the kiddies. Which we did. It caused some unpleasantness amongst the relations. The Sanitary had specified that this was one of the repairs that would have to be done. One of the other repairs was the toilet, which I referred to earlier, which never was done, by the way. To cut a long story short, this room was never repaired.

One morning we got up and it was a lovely shining morning, and I wandered in there. And the children pointed out there were some flowers on the wall. I just chuckled at it. I took no notice and I came back in here. I said to Marjorie, 'Good God, those children have got a fantastic imagination. One of them just came up to me and said there was flowers on the wall.' She turned round and said, 'Well, there is.' I went into the front room, and sure enough it was. It wasn't flowers, it was fungus. In fact it was toadstools, big ones too. About two inches in diameter. I thought this was the absolute end. We were disgusted, fed up, the whole thing was getting on my nerves and Marjorie's. We were right up to the brim.

The landlord came, and I said, 'This wall, Ted, can you do anything with it?' He said, 'Well, you plaster it and I'll pay you for it.' So I said: 'That will do.' So we plucked these toadstools off the wall. We kept our fingers off them because I'm sure they were poisonous

and threw them away. There was a dozen or so, they were flourish-
ing. The sun had got onto the wall and was making them flourish. A
lovely pink colour they were. Anyway I chopped them off, chopped
the wall down. It was soaked. The brick was saturated. I got a pal
to fix me up with some plaster and I slapped it on. I'll probably
have to do the opposite wall too, because it's riddled with it. I
know what it is. It's the chimney-pot. You see we never light a
fire in there, it's an open chimney-pot, and when it rains it just
pours in. It pours straight down this chimney-pot. It's running
down the stack and soaking out towards the outer wall. The floorboards were done two or three years ago and they were processed
with some stuff that this repair chap put on. They were old boards
and he processed them with some stuff to stop the damp, but I can
show you a spot right now where the things have gone again with
damp, rot, in fact I put my foot through it the other day.

My wife has always lived in one of these houses ever since she was
born. She has never known anything different, except the one-room
flat we moved into when we first got married. These houses are
crippled with damp. I think that was the reason why, when she was
a baby, she had a chronic chest complaint. She was under the doctor for seven years. She had sun-ray treatment and all sorts of things.
She has never got rid of this. I should imagine that whilst we are in
this house and there is a constant damp atmosphere she will never
get rid of it. But it's a case of 'Keep your chin up, keep smiling and
carry on.' Because there's not a fat lot we can do.

As regards the children we've been very very keen. The slightest
cough, and off to the doctor's immediately. The little girl had
bronchitis. It may not have been bronchitis, but she was always
very chesty. In fact now the three of them, if they cough, it really
rattles. Like I say, the children's bedroom is damp. My eldest lad
sleeps about three-foot away from a damp wall. There's nothing we
can do about it. There's nowhere else we can put him. If we move
him into our rooms, that's also damp. So we gain nothing. Generally
their health is pretty good, because we keep on top of them. They
have medical checks every six months. I do this. I admit I nag
Because I know that if it gets hold of them that's it. They're only
young and they can easily be crippled by some chest complaint.

We did try to get a council house. We had roughly been in the
house two years and we had had our eyes opened. We were very
upset we had moved into such a dilapidated place and we sat down

and decided we'd make plans. We called in the Sanitary and they suggested that we write off to the Housing Manager. Anyway we did this. But unfortunately it seemed the letter had gone to the Health Department. Some mistake had been made somewhere along the line. So we tried again, later on, about two years ago. We wrote off. No, I think you inquired for us, Mr Allaun. There was no record of us on the housing list. Nevertheless they replied with full forms obviously entitling us to council accommodation of some sort. We filled these out, prepared to live anywhere, within reason, of course: Irlam, Eccles, Little Hulton and Walkden. Council house preferred. Would move into a maisonette or flat, if nothing else was possible.

So we sent this off in high hopes that we would receive something within twelve months. We were excited about it. That was two years ago and since then we've never heard a peep. Nobody's been round to the door. We've had no return of mail, no suggestion of a movement, no suggestion of the house coming down. As far as I know these houses are up for another seven years and if they live that long they will have done damn well. But it's come to that point now, as regards going for a council house, I think it's out. Because there's no priority for anybody. Only those in the demolition areas get rehoused. You are just a herd of cattle. You're in the line. You're in a filing cabinet. Your name is stuck at the back. If you get one you're damn lucky. It's just a case of waiting. You're at their mercy. It's as simple as that.

We did try somewhere else. You may remember showing me a letter from a couple that had moved out to Bacup. It seems they were very pleased with it. We said we would be prepared to move.

We received a letter from the Bacup Housing Manager saying yes. We were acceptable and would we be prepared to go up on a specified date. This was fine. It was a council house, three bedrooms, bathroom, indoor toilet. Everything you said we would get. So my wife and I went up there. I didn't know where Bacup was or how far it was. That was the first disappointment, because it is on the clock actually twenty miles. And at this time when we had this opportunity to go to Bacup I had just got into a new job which is paying rather well. It's paying a helluva sight more than I have ever earned before. The first thing that came into my mind was that I'm going to lose this job. I can't afford to because of the money etcetera. Anyway we gave it a try and we went up to Bacup. My wife was a little dubious about it, though I pointed out the benefits as regards a bathroom and inside toilet. We discussed this at length. The job situation was the difficulty. I called in at the Bacup Labour Exchange and at the time there was nothing there which would support us, to pay the rent and buy food.

From Bacup to this house is twenty miles. From Bacup to Rochdale it's seven miles. Difficult of access. Because the buses are very contrary. I did inquire. It would mean possibly train fare, buses from Rochdale to Davyhulme, which is where I work.

You can add another ten miles onto the twenty, which makes it sixty miles a day. We worked this out and we couldn't afford it.

What are our present hopes? The position has arrived where, unfortunately, Marjorie has been forced out to work. We have decided we will try to go in for a house. I doubt if it will be anything special. It'll probably be two bedrooms and a bathroom and a front and back garden, which is what we want to start with. Whether we'll succeed or not I don't know, because plans can be uprooted in a flash. But this is what we want to try and do, if we can pay for it.

When we first got married my working position was semi-skilled at an electrical company, plastic moulding. The wage was very bad, about £9 a week flat, plus about £4 a week bonus. With overtime, on top line, I was getting about £19 a week, the taking home wage being roughly £15. This was five years ago, and I was bringing home this wage for a good three years. Later we got a £3 wage increase. I left there and went to work for a television repair company, where the wage was pretty much the same, for a year to eighteen months. So I would say that up to nine months ago my take home wage would average less than £20 a week. So, on a wage like that, it was out of the question to try to buy my own house.

As a matter of fact I did try to do this on that wage and I was advised not to bother because of my low income. I asked an insurance company if they could help me out and they said the best thing I could do was to try and improve my wage first.

Now I work a forty hour week and ten hours overtime. That brings my wage up to £37, and I bring home £30 after insurance, tax, fares and dinners. But I've only been earning this over the past nine months. It's a good job, working for a big firm of civil engineers on a sewage works. But I don't know how much longer this contract will take before the job is finished. I think with this extra money

I'm earning we should be able to afford some little accommodation somewhere. I sincerely hope so, for the kiddies' sake, if for no-one else.

I can only plead pure ignorance about how much deposit I'd need to pay, as it's way out of my sphere. I'm very ignorant on this subject of buying property. I'll probably call on my father to help me out with this problem. I've asked certain friends at work and they advise me it's the best thing to do. But some of them have said it can be a helluva millstone round your neck and that you never shake it off.

However, this is a situation where we are prepared to do anything to get out. So long as it doesn't run us into debt and we finish off worse. But this is what we are prepared to do to get out of this house and this street.

JOHN MURRAY: *Nine into one won't go*

Gorton, the classical engineering and railway belt of Manchester. Today the rows of diminutive two-ups, two-downs are deteriorating fast. The Murrays live in a typical back street. No bath, hot water or inside toilet. Their house, however, is owner-occupied, and even at a glance from outside you can tell it is better looked after than the land-lord-owned houses in the street. It has been repainted and, though the door opens straight onto the pavement, as in the other houses, Mr Murray has put in an inner door to prevent draughts and to provide a little hall.

John, the eldest son, aged twenty-two, is home on leave from the British Army of the Rhine. He wears a bright purple satin Cossack shirt. As he talks, his wife rocks their four months old baby girl to sleep in her pram.

Living in the house there's nine people. Six sleep upstairs and three sleep down. You've seen the two rooms upstairs. They're 12 feet by 14 feet. In one room sleep my two sisters who are thirteen and fourteen in one double bed. Next to them is the baby's cot. And next to the baby is my wife in a single bed. There's no room between them. You have to climb over the bed to lie down. In the next bedroom there's my two brothers. Downstairs we have my Gran – she's seventy-nine – and my own parents. They sleep in the one room, partly divided by a small partition. There isn't another room. My mother and father have been sleeping downstairs in this collapsible bed for fourteen years now.

We've been living in this house for seventeen years. My father became an owner-occupier, paying off the purchase price in instalments. They've been trying to get a council house for seven years, but because they are owner-occupiers the council refused. The parents offered to hand over the house to the council lock stock and barrel for nothing in exchange for a council house. This was turned down on grounds no one can understand. The house is grossly overcrowded and we tried to get a move on for this reason – still no joy.

I'm in the Army at the moment. I joined for six years. That leaves me eighteen months to do. Then I'll come out. My wife has tried for a council house. On the first time of writing to the Council she got no reply from them whatsoever. She left it about a month and applied again. The official told her: 'If you haven't heard by now you might as well take it you've been crossed off the list.' More recently we've taken the matter up with Ken Marks, the MP for Gorton. He's tried on our behalf and there's an inspector from the Council coming to see us, although we don't know what the outcome of this is going to be.

We've no hopes of getting a home in Germany. At the moment the position there is quite terrible. There's over two thousand married people in my garrison, with only two hundred married quarters. And that's for all ranks, not just us junior ranks. From colonel down there's still a great waiting list. There's quite a lot of the lads whose wives are living with their in-laws or whose wives are living in hostels. Nothing can be done about it by the Army. They just leave it to us. Even the officers have an eight months waiting list. It's the same all over Germany. You see they have pulled all the forces out of the Far East.

I was stationed in Colchester before I went abroad. The wife was eight months pregnant when I got my posting order. On the day of my move she was practically nine months gone. I had applied for an extension. I was told I couldn't get one because Germany is an 'accompanied' post – even though she couldn't accompany me there because there was no accommodation.

So my wife was turned out of her quarters in Colchester. After the one month's notice. We managed to get her put up with some friends of ours in Colchester till she went into hospital to have Diane. She lived with friends for a month after the baby was born. Then I came home on leave and my parents travelled down to Colchester and took us back here.

For army wives there's no room now, either in places like Colchester or in Germany, after this big pull-out of servicemen from the Far East. So there's practically no quarters available, as they are trying to cram them back into the quarters originally allocated for the forces in England and Germany.

In the newspapers of garrison towns like Colchester there has been quite a few cases. There was one case of a woman, who had three children, including a little child of eighteen months. When her husband was posted overseas she was told she had to get out of her quarters. Her husband applied for quarters or an extension, but they refused it. After he had gone abroad his wife wrote to the *Colchester Gazette*, which gave the story a big front-page billing. After that his wife was allowed to retain the quarters for nine months. But the husband got a rifting. He was reprimanded because it's against the rules to write to the papers.

There's hostel accommodation in Corsham. But it's sub-standard and only meant for short stays of up to three months. There's quite a long waiting list to get into the hostels. I think the only thing the Army can do now is to build more quarters. If the housing situation doesn't improve I don't see how people are going to stay in the Army. The recruiting drive is really going to go down the drain.

My parents have no privacy, living and sleeping downstairs. My brothers and sisters are always running down. Since we had the centre wall knocked down we call all of it the living-room. Now we've got my Gran living with us and sleeping in the same room, we've no privacy at all. My parents' bed is just a fold-up bed. They used to sleep in a bed my father made, which drops into the wall. It's not much bigger than a single bed.

My parents brought this up with the Council and offered to show them the conditions. But still nothing has been done about it. When they applied for a house and were refused they were put on the waiting list. They were put on the 'R' list. These are people who own their own houses but who will never get a house as long as they are on that list. We know some people who were tenants of a house, not owner-occupiers, in an appalling condition. The houses round here generally are in an appalling condition. They applied for and got a flat on the new estate outside Manchester in Hattersley, within a fortnight of applying. You see they were just rented tenants.

My wife and young child are sleeping in the same room as my two sisters. With the child being only four months old and having teething problems its waking my sisters up. On the other hand the sisters, being only adolescents, thirteen and fourteen, are waking the child up during the day.

The general situation is quite terrible. It causes conflict. The members of the family have started arguing amongst themselves now. When my Gran came to stay it got worse. She's seventy-nine and has got the old Victorian ideas of bringing up children and tries to enforce them in the house. Whereas my wife, and also my mother and father, have got pretty modern ideas. Gran bickers with them and causes rows. I don't think any two families living together in one house can get on – and we've nearly three families here. It's just human nature.

My wife applied to the Welfare Department to get into a hostel. They told her that the only time she could get into a hostel here was when the parents put her out into the street and she was just wandering around without a roof. But even though we may get on each other's backs we stick together as a family. They wouldn't put her out.

We tried to rent a landlord's house. We even went out as far as the Heaton Park area. We tried a house there, till the people next door advised us not to rent it because the family who had lived there previously hadn't slept upstairs for sixteen years because of the dampness. After we had refused the house for that reason someone else moved in the following week. We'd have liked to buy a house. But to get a mortgage on my pay is practically impossible. We can only go on waiting now. I've only eighteen months left to do in the Army. So I hope to get out and then apply to the Council for my own house; or buy my own house.

John's wife: The times I've been down to the Housing Officer. I've given up hope. It makes you disconsolate.

EILEEN ECKERSLEY: *Letter to an MP*

August 13, 1971

Dear Sir,

I wonder if you can help me as I am quite desperate to get out of this house, which I and my family have occupied for twenty-eight years.

I have written reams of letters, made endless calls to the housing people, and I have been on the housing list for twelve years, and I am still no further on. I try to make the best of what I've got, but it cannot make up for no bathroom and no indoor toilet.

My husband does not have the best of health and we applied to his doctor for a Medical Cert., hoping this would help, but it was no use.

Then there was all this talk about applying for a grant to modernise your home, i.e., 'We will help you to install a bathroom and indoor toilet'. We have a *small* room upstairs and so I applied, but, no, my application was turned down again.

Last year in the very depths of winter my husband and I were off work ill. When we wanted to use the toilet we had to leave a warm bedroom and go to the bottom of a wet, cold, backyard – now I ask you! I don't want to get really bitter about this. But you or anyone else can visit my home at any time and you will see the conditions under which we live.

These are the facts:

Twenty-eight years fully paid up rent book.

Sick husband.

Boy at Grammar School, nowhere to entertain his friends.

Nowhere to put my daughter and her husband when they come to visit.

So please, I beg of you, do your very best for me and I shall always remember you in my prayers, with gratitude. Please do *not* put us in the skyscraper flats.

Yours most sincerely,

Eileen Eckersley

2. In transition

EDWARD PETERS · STAN FITTON

EDWARD PETERS: *Life in the demolition zone*

Davey Street was never a rose garden. It was just a long street of brick setts with begrimed terrace houses opening straight onto the pavement. The only other things to see were factory chimneys, a cinder croft and a few lamp posts.

Today, however, it looks far, far, worse. It resembles a battlefield. For clearance is beginning. Only five families remain in Davey Street, and though rehousing is in sight their living conditions have in the meanwhile become much worse than ever. They have been left behind.

Edward Peters, a railwayman, lives at number 28 with his four year old boy, whose custody he has been given. He owns the house and his insurance agent says about it: 'There's not a nicer kept house in the area.' On either side the houses are empty, their doors and windows covered with corrugated iron to prevent access, awaiting the demolition gangs.

I bought this house back in 1953. Then, two years ago, it was CPO'd. That's to say the Corporation took it over under a Compulsory Purchase Order. I've since been paying 47 new pence rent each week, plus 58 new pence rates. They told me I'd be out of the house and in council accommodation within eighteen months.

I've tried to keep it nice, plastering the walls myself, wallpapering and buying new furniture. But it's hopeless. I'm up to here about it.

There's a hole in the empty house on one side. Kids got in through this hole and broke the water pipe. I was flooded out because the water accumulated in that house and came through the walls into my kitchen. As this was a main water pipe it also cut off my water supply.

The house on the other side is supposed to be boarded up too.

But it isn't properly blocked. The other week I found two men inside, stripping it of lead and wood. There are people who live on the pickings of these houses as soon as they are empty. They sell the timber and lead.

We've also discovered kids in the rafters of one of these empty houses, busy setting fire to it. It's lucky we haven't all been killed. It wasn't till I'd gone to the Council several times that they put the corrugated iron across the doors. But not before vandals had wrecked the house next door and pulled the floorboards up. During the day I'm at work and the little boy is with relations. One evening I got home and found we had had burglars in our own house.

I get the mice and beetles from the empty houses on both sides. You see that three-piece suite. I paid £100 for that. But look at the hole the mice have made underneath it.

The backyard wall collapsed. This has now been rebuilt by the Corporation workmen.

My house became much wetter when the two houses on either side became unoccupied. You can see that the new wallpaper I put on is all peeling off.

It rains into the bedroom where the boy and I sleep. But worse than that is the crack in one wall, stretching straight down from the roof to the ground. 'Not dangerous', they say at the Town Hall.

On the other side of the house they rehoused the people who lived there because it was unfit to live in. The Council put a young couple in this house and they were there for eighteen months. Then they got a council flat.

As I say, I was up to here, what with the burglars and the fire and the flooding and the mice and the damp. So I went down to the housing offices and gave them twenty-four hours to find me somewhere to go to. I'd filled in the application form three years ago and hadn't had a single offer. Their attitude seems to be 'Oh, you're all right. Yours is a nice house.' So when I went down to the offices they offered me a re-let. But it was filthy, with human dirt on the floor. It needed redecorating from top to bottom. They would have redecorated it, but I said, 'I'm not taking my kiddie in there.' They'll have to offer me something better than that.

STAN FITTON: *In Limbo*

Inside the tiny, but brightly decorated and furnished living-room of the Fittons. Councillor Stan Fitton is tubby, pink-complexioned, fifty-one, balding. He looks like a cross between a bishop and a prosperous butcher. In fact he is a skilled engineer. His house, along with all the others in the long streets of the neighbourhood, has no bath, hot water or inside wc and is due for demolition. Slum clearance has already reached a third of the district and is approaching street by street. As a result, the normal housing troubles are intensified. Since Stan lives in the heart of his ward he often finds four or five neighbour-constituents queuing up on his doorstep for advice on their problems. They even delay his getting to work on time in the morning, waylaying him as he leaves home.

He worries the Town Hall officials into taking action. Because his grass roots are so strong he often knows more about the conditions than they do.

On the walls are photographs of his two sons in their degree day cloaks and gowns. Today they are both university lecturers with wives and children of their own.

He and his wife, Sylvia, have their own housing problem, though their fight is for others. They look at Chief, their big, black Newfoundland dog, knowing that he will have to be put to sleep when they are moved into new council property. And they will probably only get a one-bedroom flat, which means they won't be able to accommodate their children when they come to visit them.

When an area like this begins to get demolished, first, the Housing Department, which has undertaken a survey, starts to allocate the keys for the new homes. Unfortunately they can only allocate the keys for what properties they have available. From my experience I have noticed that they haven't got a proper assortment of properties ready to let.

For example they build a block of flats which contain only one or two bedrooms. So there's no three- and four-bedroom accommodation available. This means that those with big families have got to wait till this is there for them. On the other hand – just as it is here at present – it can happen that they have no one-bedroom accommodation ready. So there's some elderly people who have been waiting nine months for rehousing after clearance had started round them, because they want to remain in the district they have been residing in. There has been one-bedroom flats available, but it's been in multi-storey blocks, and these elderly people would rather have the low-rise development down here.

It means that these people, being old and not having a lot to say for themselves, are left behind, because they are not in a position to defend themselves as they should be. In a previous clearance area people were left for twelve months. In that case it was people with large families. So small children were suffering the worst possible conditions.

They are not left in a row of terraced property, but just odd houses here and there. When the winter comes on they have the protection taken away from them of a house on each side. Slates are taken off the roofs. There's leaking water pipes where people have come and stolen the lead piping. Consequently the house walls are being sprayed with water, causing dampness in the houses of those who remain. There was a case in a street near here where the water was cut off and the lady was left without any water at all for eleven weeks.

When I got on to the health authorities they told me that in certain circumstances, where it was too expensive, they wouldn't get the water put back. That lady had to go to her mother's for water, nearby. So it means this: if your predicament is too expensive to put right, in view of coming demolition, you are going to be left in these conditions.

As demolition takes place the rats, mice and other vermin get driven out of their old haunts into houses still occupied either in those streets or in neighbouring ones. They even get them in the bedrooms, there are so many of them. You didn't usually have this affliction previously.

Then you've got the vandals who come breaking windows. You've got people who come squatting in the areas, because they are not demolished quick enough. You've also got children setting places on fire, because you know what children are. They get into any open property. They get themselves into danger. You even have instances where you have to have empty houses bricked up before they demolish them, for the safety of the children.

The streets were being neglected, because the authorities thought: 'It's a demolition area, why should we waste time cleaning them?' The houses were left with rotten old furniture in them, which began to stink. People come and dump refuse in the empty places. Now – since we had the mothers' demonstration – they clear each property out and remove all the old junk and stale food. They are kept cleaner now.

In the Number Two clearance area the larger families were left there for a long time. The children were falling down grids, because vandals had stolen the cellar grids and coal chute grids for the iron, which they weigh in. The lamps are broken in the street. So it's completely dark. And they go out and fall down these grids. They are going to the hospital with cuts and for stitches.

You can take it that here nearly every other person who has been left on their own has been robbed. They don't dare leave their home for a minute, because, if they do, there's somebody in. They steal money from the meters, clocks, televisions, or whatever they find. Very few get caught. So you don't know who's doing it. There's no neighbours to see anyone going in, because these houses are in isolation. They can be entered in daylight. It's so simple. So, as I say, at one stage or another, nearly half of them have been robbed.

The conditions become terrible. You see, you get a deterioration in the property. In clearance areas it seems the Corporation don't want to deal with any problems. I'll give you an instance. I've asked for guardrails on the pavement in a street not far from here. Because it's a future clearance area I've been told they won't spend money on this. But these people are still expected to pay the rates. So it's not only demolition areas but future demolition areas too. If a street lamp gets broken round here I can't get it replaced. So the people suffer in lots of ways that you don't realise. I could show you areas completely in blackness at night. But people are still living there. You can understand the Corporation saying: 'We can't keep repairing vandalised property, because of the expense.' But you must consider the people who've still got to live in these places.

As soon as a new area is declared as due for clearance you have a constant stream of people coming to see you to see if they can get away quick. For the children get to work quickly and it becomes intolerable to live in these conditions.

In this ward the women got that fed up with waiting to be rehoused, when only the couples without children or small families had been found new homes, we decided on a march to the Town

Hall and to demand to see the housing committee, to see what could be done. It was a Tory controlled Council at the time, and still is, though I'm a Labour councillor and a member of the housing committee. So about sixty to seventy of them marched down to the Town Hall with their children and with prams. They would not be turned away from the Town Hall until they had seen the housing committee.

So the committee decided to meet a deputation of five of the ladies who had come from the area, to listen to their complaints. Eventually we got things moving. It had some effect. Some of them got properties which were re-lets. Here we've only had multi-storey property, and there has been a lot of resentment against it. We've not had enough mixed development to accommodate these people.

So these ladies didn't mind at all being moved into re-lets rather than into new flats. They were satisfied because these houses had the amenities they hadn't got in their own homes.

The Council pushed the building contractors a bit. And as soon as a few properties became available they let them in small units instead of waiting for bigger numbers as they had done before. Say twelve at a time, whereas before they waited for more to become available at a time. Now they don't wait for a complete unit to be finished. As soon as one low-rise flat becomes available they let it.

You've got to live in these areas to understand the problems. If you're sitting on the outside and looking in you don't really get a true picture of what's happening to these people. At one period the fire brigade was down in this area two and three times a day, through vandals setting property on fire. They are kids, doing it just for the love of seeing the houses on fire.

The Council takes too big a stretch at once. Some families or old people get left behind because the suitable accommodation isn't there. Isolated, one in one street and perhaps two or three in another. There's an old chap of eighty-odd left behind just now in Martha Street.

Some of these old people – I quite understand 'em – want to stay in this area. And the property won't be ready for months. Right through the winter. They won't go in a multi-storey block in another part of the town. They'd sooner stay where they have lived all their lives. The housing department should have been getting so many one-bedrooms ready, so many two-bedrooms and so many three- and four-bedrooms. So they would have been available for letting at a similar time. Then you could move a whole street. There's a piece of ground near here where they couldn't start on the roads and sewers because they were held up on account of somebody still living there. But they could have started on another area which had been cleared.

The answer is to get on with the building quicker. The Council won't leave any new property vacant because they want the income from the rent. But they seem to be doing just one particular kind of development at a time instead of getting a mixed development. There's some one-bedroom flats they're building near here which have been stopped for months. If they had put more workmen onto that job they would then have been able to move the old people who have been left behind on their own.

What it means is that they shouldn't start clearing an area until they have enough alternative accommodation available. But the difficulty of the Council is that they don't want to keep new housing empty because of loss of rent revenue. If they started a bigger building scheme and a smaller demolition scheme we'd have the properties becoming available at once, instead of in a dribble.

We've a new development going up, with a district heating scheme. They'll be good houses. But here again they have made no provision for old people and disabled people. There's a lady with multiple sclerosis who's been left on her own for nine months in that condition. They've now moved her into this new property. Now she's in they are going to start altering the doors, instead of altering the property at the time they knew they were going to put this lady into it. And I'm almost sure there's no provision being made for old people in the next stage.

We contacted the MP and he raised it in Parliament. The reply we got was that the Government had no jurisdiction over local authorities. But really they have. Because it still rests with the Government to see that the needs of the people are served properly. And that means giving the local authorities the funds to carry out the work, which they won't do. Without the funds to carry the work out we're going to be struggling all the time. Money is always the cause of the trouble. Money is more important than people. Whilst we've got this position we'll always be in the same boat.

Most of these people who are left behind are people who won't speak up for themselves or defend themselves. It's that they have got old and can't chase about. Some of them are crippled or confined to their homes. And an elderly person who goes out to work can't afford to lose time to go chasing to the Housing Department. But those mothers I mentioned were forceful and were able to kick up a fuss. I feel really sorry for the old people. I've got a list here I'm going to see the Housing over today. What I have to do is to get them rehoused as quickly as possible. When they come to see you, you can help to make arrangements for them to be fitted into re-let properties. Sometimes the Housing Department assists you if it's the constituent's turn. A re-let is a council property which has been lived in by another tenant. They are standard properties with baths and inside lavatories.

We've moved some people to overspill. But if they work in town they have to face a bill of thirty-odd shillings a week for bus fares. So that, on top of the increased rent, plus taxation, it leaves you very little to play with. You can't get an increase in wage to recompense you for this. So you have to do without a lot of things in life which you normally enjoy. You can't go out like you used to do.

We're going to be moved ourselves. I'm not worried, because these properties are old. They are past their best. The walls are buckled, the floors have dry rot in them. There's no bath in the house. We've got an outside toilet. I will, at least, have an indoor toilet and bathroom. They are quite good properties when you move. It's worth it. We'll be going in a flat.

Sylvia Fitton: They come round asking you what kind of property you want. And in the next breath they tell you the only kind of property you can have. I think it's very arrogant and presumptuous of them to tell you what your requirements are. Once you move you are going to be there for the rest of your life and you want somewhere where you are going to be happy.

A couple without children are automatically entitled to a one-bedroom flat. They are only giving houses to families. Well, I can understand that. But I think they should give you a chance of a low-rise flat. They don't take into account the adaptability of people, or what condition their nerves are in. I personally am very high strung. I couldn't go in a lift if you paid me £5 a week to live in a multi-storey. Just recently I've been dreaming about them. Even if I was on the bottom floor I have dreams that the rest of the property is crowding in on me and I can't get out in time. It would be impossible for me to go in a flat.

I've a mother with heart trouble. In two or three years I expect she will have to come and live with me. So I want to move into a two-bedroom so I'll be prepared for that eventuality. And I'm not prepared to move into new property and buy new carpets and then have to move out again.

Stan Fitton: They come round with the forms and ask where you would like to go. Then they say you can only go here and here and here. So you are restricted to what they wish to give you.

Take a married couple with a family who have got married and are living away from home. Sometimes they come to stay with you for a week-end. Both my sons are married. One lives two hundred miles away. Now if he comes to visit me down here and wishes to stay here, if I'm put in a one-bedroom flat I'll be unable to put them up. I don't see why people should be made to accept a one-bedroom where they have sons or daughters who come to visit them occasionally, which they are entitled to do. The Council are asking you to become a hermit, more or less, and keep them away from your home. This is wrong. I don't see why you should be made to accept a one-bedroom when you're already living in a house with two or three bedrooms. You should at least have the additional bedroom for anyone coming to visit you and wanting to be put up for the night. Fancy chasing round at midnight to look for accommodation for the visitor, or having to put them up in the lounge on the floor.

They tell you you can have a two-bedroom multi-storey, but not a two-bedroom low-rise. We're not asking for houses. We agree that families should be placed in houses, but they are telling people too much what they *must* have.

Sylvia Fitton: We're quite willing to have the dog put to sleep. We think a lot about him but we understand you can't let a dog stand in your light. Their span of life is very limited.

And another point I've noticed is that, between people who have been neighbours all their life, it's causing a bone of contention, watching one another to see what kind of accommodation they're getting, and why he's getting it. They say, 'I'll see why I can't get it. There's something underhanded going on.' They are setting people against one another. And this is all adding to the neurosis which is becoming more prevalent in the area. They are all at one another's throats.

People say, 'How has she got this? I'm going down to find out and they had better tell me why.' This is all you can hear when you go out.

Stan Fitton: When they find somebody else has got rehoused before them they start creating at the Housing Department. Which you can understand when they are living in conditions like this.

Sometimes the officials cause unnecessary difficulties. We were being told that so many properties were available and nobody would take them. Yet I know there's ninety people in this particular clearance area that would have accepted some of these properties that the official claimed they had to let. But they've not been offered anywhere yet. So they create unnecessary unrest among people by making silly statements at times.

I'll admit they have a difficult job to do. But, by the same rule, their job finishes at five o'clock at night – and your job starts when you finish work. Our job's more difficult than theirs, because we've got to explain away to people who come asking questions as to why they are doing these things. And you are not in that office all day finding out *why* they are doing them. You can't, at times, understand why they do what they do.

Take, for instance, the case of a lady there who has been waiting quite a while for a place to be decorated before she goes into it. As a result this lady is holding up work on the drains and sewers in the next stage, because her present house is right in the middle of where they have started digging. If you are going into a re-let you expect it to have been made suitable. If the person who has been in those premises before has left it in a bad state it's got to be repaired, and it's only natural that it's got to be decorated for the person who is going in. The department will take a list of all the repairs that need doing. Then it will be maybe three months before they start work on them.

This is something that shouldn't happen. Because we've got our own building maintenance department. They were going to sack forty painters not so long ago because they had no work – and yet we can't get the places decorated. So what's going wrong? It's bad management, and lack of co-operation between departments.

I get on the 'phone and ask: 'Have you put in an order for this?' They say: 'Oh, yes.' I 'phone the building maintenance department and say: 'Why haven't you done this job?' They tell me: 'We've got no order.' You can never find out who's telling the truth. You can only accept a person's word. They might be both right. They might have sent an order in and it's got mislaid. But this happens too often. Yet when I get on to the building maintenance manager he sends his men round right away.

Why should somebody like a councillor from outside who's not being paid to do a job have to tell them what to do? They are being paid to run the job properly. When an order is given I expect it to be carried out, the same as if I'm told to do a job at work I'm expected to do it. Something goes wrong somewhere. And this is happening all too often.

3. Making a new home

DOUGLAS CLARK · STEPHEN RYAN · KATHLEEN RYAN
SAM SILLARS · ADA GIBSON · MAURICE LINDLEY

DOUGLAS CLARK: *Our own bedroom*

*After seventeen years the Clark family has found a new home. Now
they live in a semi-detached Salford council house, overlooking the
green expanse of a large recreation ground. Four poplar trees, planted
by the previous tenant, grow in the back garden, with another poplar in
the front.*

*Douglas Clark is a dustman. He is slightly built, wearing a jersey
with sleeves rolled up, revealing tatooed arms, and looks younger than
his thirty-six years.*

*He and his quieter, more reserved wife, proudly show me round a
house that they have, in a few months, turned into a model home. What
is most striking is the neatness. Even the children's bedrooms are in
apple-pie order, with their books arranged in orderly fashion on the
shelves. Indeed everything is so clean and tidy it might be thought that
the six children would be repressed. On the contrary they are bubbling
over with life, constantly giggling with fun.*

We got married at eighteen and lived for a few months with my
mother until we managed to get a two-up, two-down in the same
street.

My wife is a Yorkshire girl. She had a very hard childhood – her
mother died when she was very young. She had a drunken father
and a stepmother. Much of her childhood she spent in a children's
home. In fact she has started writing her own life-story. It is
because of her own experience that she is so determined our
children are not going to have the same. That is why she is insistent
on plenty of soap and water, and why she was so insistent on getting
out of the old house.

We had four of the children sleeping in one tiny room. I fixed
up two sets of bunks on top of each other. No bath, of course. So

we had to bath the children in a tin bath on the floor. My wife suffers a lot from nerves, which give her a skin trouble. With eight of us living in two bedrooms we had row after row after row. There were family arguments night after night.

For seventeen years we were on the waiting list for a council house. We applied on the grounds of my wife's health. Her skin complaint needed a daily bath. She continually went down to the housing office. They told her, 'Sorry, you have no chance.' You know in the same street there are houses kept in very different conditions inside. We suffered because we kept ours nice. If it had been scruffy maybe we would have got a council house earlier. But Mary couldn't leave it dirty. The street got worse as demolitions took place.

She used to threaten the housing people, 'If you are not going to help us I'm going to leave home.' Suddenly the news came out of the blue. Mary had been to the office and they told her, 'Nothing doing.' Then, the very next day, they offered us this house. It's about forty years old.

We've been here seven months and look at the difference it has made.

My wife and I have a bedroom on our own. For the first time for seventeen years we have got privacy. Because she has less worry her nerves are better. Her skin has cleared.

The main improvement for her was the bath, which we never had before. Naturally it suits me fine after a day's work with the dustbins. And the Council has taken the old one out of the bath-room and put in a modern one instead. It costs us two shillings extra on the rent – but it's worth it.

The children are doing well at school. Mind you, my wife never let the bad circumstances hold their education back in the old area. But now it's perfect. They can go into the little parlour to do their homework, where it's nice and quiet. The girls can have their friends in, too, and put on the recorder there, without the blaring music getting us all down. When we were in the old house they couldn't have their friends round, because with eight of us already in the room, there was nowhere for them to sit.

The two eldest girls have got their own room now, with their own wardrobe. They chose a wallpaper they liked. They've put pictures up of Stevie Wonder and the Motown Chartbusters.

We have been lucky in our next door neighbours. They are an

elderly couple – the husband is a cripple. When they heard that a family with six children was coming to live in the adjoining house they put up barbed wire between the two gardens. Yet now we've got to know each other we get on fine together.

The new house has made the four younger children happy. They have more room. They cause no trouble; get on well together; no quarrelling or fighting. They make their own beds. You'll see the photos of Georgie Best and Manchester United on their wall.

They can go out onto the playing-field with the dog. But they mostly prefer to play in their own garden. I've sown grass seed and it's come up very well.

I have put a lot of work in inside the house. Every room has been redecorated, except one, which already had very nice wall-paper. The hot-water pipes which were exposed in the sitting-room have been boxed in with hardboard and then repapered.

We haven't been away for a holiday since we went five years ago to a caravan near Blackpool. This year my fortnight on the rota was very early – at the end of April and the beginning of May. However, I didn't complain because it suited me, as we had just gone into the new house, which gave me a good chance to get things improved.

Mind you, we reckon it costs us £6 to £7 a week more than it used to before we moved. The rent is £4.45 a week compared with £1 previously. Then there are the bus fares for the children to and from the new school – and they all come home for dinner. The two oldest go out to work in an office. It costs £3 a week between the two of them just for dinners and bus fares.

My flat wage is £18, plus a bonus for doing so many bins. Including the bonus and overtime working I clear about £20 a week after insurance and stoppages.

My wife gets up at five o'clock in the morning. She works from six o'clock to eight o'clock as a cleaner at a big firm. Then she works at the same firm in the evenings from five o'clock to eight o'clock, for five and a half days a week. She is anaemic, so she gets very tired with it.

We stay in at night and watch television. It's a nice home to stay in. I may go out for a drink at the week-end.

The two oldest girls had their childhood in an old two-up, two-down. It's too late now for them. But my wife says about the younger ones, 'They've got what I never had.'

2*

STEPHEN RYAN: *A student at home*

Stephen is eighteen and just starting to grow a moustache. His life has changed in two ways within twelve months. First he has come with his family to live in a new block of council maisonettes. Secondly, he recently won four A levels and as a result has just spent his first term at university.

I went to a primary school in a poor part of the city. Then I went to a technical high school until I was sixteen, when that school was amalgamated into a grammar technical school. I did my arts subjects in the sixth form, and then, having got my 'A' levels, I was lucky enough to get a university place.

Till I was sixteen I lived in a corner house in a terraced block of houses. This house was originally a shop, but, by the time we had it, it wasn't really a shop. The living accommodation was front-room, living-room, a rather thin, long kitchen and two bedrooms. There was an outside toilet, no bathroom, and a large cellar, which was very damp.

We had no hot water or geyser. We had to heat all our water on a gas-stove. After you were seven or eight there was no chance of having a bath because that meant using a tin bath, which was rather inconvenient. You just had to wash yourself all over. Fortunately, as soon as I went to a secondary school there were showers. I was lucky enough to be at a school with a swimming bath. So I didn't have any hygienic problems that way. I could at least get a good wash all over once a week.

My mum didn't have a washer, which meant that she had to go every week to a launderette. Sometimes I used to take overalls and other things to the launderette on a Saturday afternoon. You had to dry them in the yard. When it was wet you had to take 'em in. You could hang them round the house on clothes racks and put them in front of the coal fire.

I only studied particularly hard in my last two years at school. Before that there was quite a problem, because to do your homework it was obviously very difficult to do it in the living-room. So the best way to do it was in the bedroom. In fact if my brother hadn't gone to the university before I did there would have been a real problem, because then there would have been two of us doing homework at the same time. But in the bedroom it tended to be cold. So often I was obliged to do it downstairs, which was rather distracting. When I was a bit older I used to do my homework downstairs after my parents had gone to bed. That way it was very quiet. That meant staying up to, say, midnight.

As for friends, there was only one lad from my primary school who went to the technical school, whom I knew. So all the friends I had at school faded away, because I didn't see them so often. There weren't many at the grammar technical school coming from my area. I suppose I was looked on a bit differently by my old friends. There's very few of my friends from the primary school whom I know particularly well now.

Then our street was demolished. Our family accepted the first key we were offered, which was for here. We've got three bedrooms in this maisonette and a kitchen and one living-room. It's certainly better for studying in, because two of the bedrooms are large ones. So my brother and I used to sleep in one of the large bedrooms and we turned the smaller one into a storeroom-cum-study-cum-place to keep your books in. So it meant I had a room for the first time specifically for studying. It's not really warmer. This maisonette is on two floors. The central heating consists of a unit on the bottom floor. Upstairs any real heating has to come from an electric fire, or hot-water-bottle.

We had an electric fire in the bedroom in our old house. But it didn't make much difference there. The house was very damp. In the cellars the walls were wringing with water. In the kitchen it was literally impossible to paper the walls. The wallpaper used to hang off an inch or so. In the upstairs you got rain in, particularly in our bedroom. The electric fire wasn't sufficient to counteract the damp cold. Even more so as the rooms were quite big and high, so you had a lot to heat up. You could only feel any warmth by sitting straight in front of the electric fire.

I get the impression that most of the students I meet haven't much idea of the conditions like this, particularly, of course, because they mostly come from the suburbs. They have rarely seen even the outsides of this kind of house.

We didn't have any difficulty in finding a place to play as a lad, because our house was right on the corner of a park. We used to go in there to play football and cricket. It also had swings and things like that. I was a big reader and the nearest library was about half a mile away. And it wasn't of a particularly good quality. So I had to go to the city's central library. I was also able to supplement my reading out of the school library. But this encouraged me to buy my own books, of which I collected a couple of hundred over the years.

In the university I live in residence – on the university campus itself. The system they have isn't in fact the traditional halls of residence. You all live in a three-storey block of flats. You all have a bedroom. Then you have a common room with kitchen facilities. If you don't do your own cooking you have refectories, cafeterias where you can go in the afternoon and evening for a full meal. You can study at the desk provided in your bedroom, or in the excellent library with full studying facilities.

The rent I pay is £120 a year. And then you pay for heating, lighting and your meals. I get £430 a year grant, which is the maximum. A student has never got enough money, but it does really cover what's necessary. You can manage on it.

There's been a lot in our local newspaper about having pubs on this huge council estate where our family live. I think pubs are absolutely necessary, because people want drinks. Most council house tenants don't have cars – and you don't want people going out drinking in cars, anyway. But the vital question is that the pubs must be sited correctly. It must be terrible to live next door to a pub, especially at throwing out time on a Saturday night at eleven o'clock. And there are some pubs only ten yards away from the housing. They should plan it so that they are isolated from the major blocks of flats so there is no serious noise problem. At the same time they shouldn't be far away from any large council estate. In the same way you must put social facilities into those estates, or else they become just dead hulks. Then it does not become a community.

So I'm saying: yes, pubs – but not *too* close. Otherwise they become a nuisance. This trouble didn't tend to arise when you had a pub on the end of a terraced street, because they were much smaller pubs. Today they are building much larger pubs. They tend to have more music and more noise. On this estate they had some trouble with one particular pub where they had the microphone on excessively loud, which meant you could hear them singing away, right up to the eighteenth floor at eleven o'clock.

People come from miles away, for some reason – possibly to

meet their old friends. It creates a problem in that it tends to over-crowd pubs. The problem is that they haven't got enough pubs anyway on an estate as large as this, as yet. It would obviously be absurd to stick a wall round the estate and put up a notice saying, 'No outsiders allowed in'. Obviously lots of people are coming to see old friends and relations. That's a healthy thing. I don't see how you can object to people coming to an estate. You can't keep them out.

A university provides a very peculiar sort of insular environment. Unlike many universities ours is completely isolated from the city itself. It's two or three miles outside. It's a completely autonomous area. Occasionally you go into the town at week-ends, partly to get away from the exorbitant prices which are charged at the students' shops. So this creates a rather odd, ivory-tower atmosphere, I suppose in the tradition of Cambridge and Oxford. But even Cambridge and Oxford colleges are in the towns themselves, instead of being stuck out on a hill.

It's very pleasant having country surrounding you. I go out almost every week-end with a hiking club. To be in the fresh air is a great change.

When I was younger I enjoyed watching the all-consuming eye in the corner there, the television. I suppose I owe a lot to the terrible mass media, because from a very young age I got the habit of avidly listening to news reports and current affairs programmes. So I picked up a lot of information that perhaps otherwise I wouldn't have got. I used to play a lot of cricket in the summer, but I didn't particularly like going out into the cold and wet in winter time. I used to read a lot. Watered down science, current affairs, literature, and history. I had a consuming interest in ancient history. I used to read a lot about astronomy. I suppose I caught this off my brother who is now doing his PhD in astronomy.

I feel that both my parents – if they had ever had the opportunity – might have got to university. I had a big advantage in that my brother was already going to a university, and so he used to bring all sorts of books into the home and talk to me about things. My mother was a very wide reader and used to take a big interest in our education.

It's very convenient having this modern shopping precinct immediately across the road. My mother does her shopping there. There's little trouble from noise, because cars coming to the precinct come in the day-time, not in the evening. In the day-time it brightens the place up to have lots of people about.

Most of the people living in these maisonettes tend to like this type of property. For a start you've got an upstairs and a downstairs. They are not too high – only ten storeys or five maisonettes high. Also they are set out almost like streets. They are long blocks, not in a square unit. So kids can play along this veranda, as you might call it.

They've got a front door, which means that housewives can stand outside and talk to one another. And little kids can play along it. Though there's a problem here. There are a few small playgrounds for the under-sevens. But when you are getting into the teenages there is a big problem: where to play. There's no sporting facilities directly in this area. For playing-fields they are a lot worse off than I was in the old part.

So there's some vandalism in the area. Some of this is simply caused by the kids kicking a ball against the windows. They have nowhere else to play with it. Throughout the estate there isn't a great deal of vandalism, except in a few blocks. And mostly this is seventeen and eighteen-year-olds coming out of the pubs drunk and fighting, people who don't necessarily live here. I'm always hearing about fights on a Saturday night, but I've never seen one myself.

There hasn't been much trouble with telephone boxes. They have been placed deliberately in prominent places and they have clear glass around, so people can see what's happening inside them. This seems to be quite an effective deterrent. This talk about vandalism can be exaggerated.

KATHLEEN RYAN: *Your own front door*

Kathleen, Stephen's mother, is a short, plump, woman with a motherly, jovial look about her. There is a warm, happy and easy relationship in the Ryan family. This does not prevent her from playing an active part in the community.

At the beginning I didn't want to come to this new estate because

I was so attached to my old ward. I was born near the park. And I only moved a few yards when Dad came out of the Army and I married him. My school and church were Saint Cyprian's, which, of course, have gone now. Ordsall Hall, which is now a museum, I've scrubbed that floor and brownstoned it. I really knew the place and loved it.

When we came here I had the habit of saying, 'I feel better now my people are coming here.' I wasn't meaning that in a big way. They were my kind of people. We do feel better – all of us – now there's more of us from Ordsall here. We've tried to bring this togetherness with us. It means you never have to worry.

If a girl had a baby, my mother would see that that baby's first meal would be fish done with milk and butter that she had done and run in with to her. Anyone on our row. That was my mother. Such and such a body has had a baby. As soon as she could eat she would take this in. 'It's nice and light. She'll like it.'

This wasn't only us. It was all round us. If you had an old person in the street, they weren't left. You knew them. You went into them. We used to go away on a holiday with Saint Cyprian's Church. There would have been perhaps six or seven mothers and forty children. The parents knew they could leave them and we'd look after them.

There was a teacher in school who must have taught three generations. She's just come away now, Miss Harris. You could look at the faces and say to yourself, 'That's one of Winnie Dean's. You can see her. She's the image of old Mrs Dean.' Her mother and her grandmother would have lived in the same street. Perhaps more than half the families in the street would be relations. There was a blood tie.

Even if you didn't think about it, it must have been there. Because at the ultimate it came out, when we had to leave the district. When they were asked did they want to leave these people, they didn't. Because these people was themselves. Even if you were going to move only half a mile off that seems an awful long way away. When you got over the park it seemed a lot different to us. From there to Ellor Street, where we now are, it might have been the other end of the world.

It took me twelve months to get over coming here to this maisonette. The first three months I nearly had a nervous break-down. I really did. I was walking round here in an absolute maze.

Back at home I would only have had to look outside the door and if I had wanted a conversation I'd have had it. I would have gone into the shop and known people there. Here you didn't. Some of my neighbours had come from Ordsall. They were all being troubled by the same thing. So they were all stopping in their little shells, because out there (and she pointed to the window) wasn't what they were used to. You understand what I mean?

Now I've got to get used to this. I live here. I like all the facilities. My Stephen said to me, 'Look over there, mam. Your Uncle Jack lives over there in Sutton flats. You can see it from here, which you couldn't do before.' It was only a state of mind. I shouldn't have been strange or lonely. You know me. I can go out and talk to anybody. Now I've settled marvellously. I wouldn't move. Dad says now we should try to move to a house. But I say, after twenty-five years waiting for a house – for that's how long we were on the waiting list for a council house, and I doubt if the street hadn't been cleared if we wouldn't still be waiting for one.

My two lads, as you know, have gone off to higher education. You couldn't do anything else but back these two boys up. We had to do without. Instead of saying: 'Right, we're going to have a house,' we couldn't have done both. It wasn't a matter of losing the boys' wages – we never had them. Philip was so obviously going to go on. My husband didn't like me going to work. He was a driver which at one time was very good money. But today's money! His basic wage now is £17 a week. Which isn't very much when you think of this £4 a week rent and then your heating. Really his money doesn't cover that kind of a thing. You can't hope to save to help them out.

So I said, 'Right. Well I'll do a part-time job.' My husband didn't like it. All right, as long as I went after the children went to school, and I was back before dinner-time. It was only a few hours. And that was saved to put Philip on his way, in the first place. As you know, they want rigging out with clothes. They want money to be sure when they get there, although he's a lad who can budget well. If he's going up to Scotland, as he did, he could come home and say, 'Mam, I'm short.' Luckily he'd always been brought up that way, to manage his money. Even when we were going away I always made them save the bus fare out of their spends. They got it back again, you know, in another way. But the point was they had to help. The bus fare was their contribution to their holidays. When Philip went to university he had £12 for his robe. It may not seem much today, but Dad was only on £9 a week then.

When we went on the housing list we just wanted a house in Salford. The furthest I'd ever thought of going was Kersal, on the north side of the city. That held us back. Because on our form we just said: a house in Salford. At that time there wasn't houses available outside as there are now. I looked round and I couldn't fancy living here. I said to Dad: 'Just imagine us living in Hanky Park,' which is what this part used to be called before they cleared the area. They were absolutely different people. They seemed to have a different way of thinking to us. And they think the same way about us. When we see Ordsall people up here we wave even if we don't know each other well. And it makes the day a bit better, the fact that you've seen one of our folks.

Now that people have been here over two years I hope that a new community is forming. In some blocks of flats where they are all people who have moved together from Ordsall they are working together, like they would have done at home. They've had a trip for the kids at Christmas. They had one for the Blackpool illuminations. On this particular block where I am we're all mixed, a job lot as you might say.

The Council should keep people together and it would work a lot better. It's not right saying they don't want the same neighbours. They do want them. It's important. It happens in an emergency, as we have had two doors away from here. She has four children. One child got hurt coming out of school. Right. Someone must look after those other children. They are all toddlers. They have got to go in somewhere and be looked after. At home you would just have said, 'I've got to go to the hospital to look after her.' And then you could have forgotten those children, knowing even the tea would have been given them.

I'm beginning to enjoy it here now. I wouldn't move, I don't think. How people can say the flats are not good enough or big enough? It's so silly when you know the areas they come from. Mind you, you do have a lot of faults here. One of them is the heating. You put your heating on, and it's frozen upstairs. We have to use electric fires upstairs. This isn't all-in heating, as it's supposed to be. But we would have had to provide our own heating in the houses we came from. But I do think it's a mistake. We're paying for this over-all equipment. So why couldn't it have heated all the house? It's like when you buy a chicken. You've got the bone in any case, and what's extra is going to be meat. You've got the heating and you've got to pay for it, so you should have had the extra.

It's a lot easier in a modern maisonette. You've got hot water on tap. You've got your bathroom. You can go in it. Even if you had built a bath in the old houses it was in the cellar, which they usually were in our row, because you hadn't got a spare room. You had to find a way of filling it and emptying it. It was a lot of nuisance. It's so much easier and comfortabler now.

We've got a little back balcony. Now this is something which I think, in flats, is causing a lot of problems: that they have no front door. But here – in this type of a maisonette – it's just like a street. You can take a brush in your hand and go onto that front door and brush for a little bit, and somebody is going to come up, and you can talk to them.

Now I've got a back balcony I can sit on. Which I do. We've had a pretty fair, dry year. I usually have my morning cup of tea out on there. But in a flat you have no front door. They are all in an inside corridor. The people on Beech Court say, 'If only we had one balcony and one window we could open to be outside.' But they have no door to open outside. Because when they open the door they are still inside.

This is very important. It's very important to a lot of these women that has had nervous breakdowns. And there has been a lot of them who has. Some haven't got by the early stage. I'm the sort of person who will fight this kind of thing. I'd say to Dad, 'You come and pick me up. Don't leave me in here today.' And I've gone with him on his lorry.

I don't think the people would have had this trouble in the old place. I know I was getting upset. I've high blood pressure, which had come on through various things, ever since I had Stephen. But Dad said it was worry over when we was moving, where we was moving, that started it off, and that when we came up here I already was a little bit depressed. Also I packed in my job. The older lad was on his way then, and it wasn't necessary. So, since then, I've taken on voluntary work. It has been good for me. It takes me out to look at other people's worries.

In the flats people are going to hate it for three to six months.

I tell them all this, you know. There are only a few exceptions. I can only put it down to their being too enclosed in flats and having no front door.

All they've got is the window, and that is like a picture. They're not living in it. The front door is the main thing. Some of these women who have come from Ordsall say, 'I'll never settle.' And I say to them: 'You will settle, because we all go through this, but we all get over it.'

Whether this happens to everyone that moves anywhere, I don't know, or whether it's just peculiar to these people I know that's been so tied up with people they'd grown up with. You see they were a community. They have peculiar ties, which were suddenly broken. These same mistakes mustn't be made again. Some areas are not close knit, and it won't affect them the same. But they apply when you have an area with a lot of intermarriage and old friendships. They just smashed Ordsall up. It can never be put back together again.

A lot have gone back, now it's being rebuilt. But they have not gone back to the same Ordsall. Ordsall is now like this place. They might as well stop here, and say, 'We're going to make this work here.' Unfortunately this hasn't happened yet. I've started to try here. I've asked them if they will get together. I tell them they've done it over on Beech Court. I think we should try to get together over something for the children. If we only get one thing going that'll get them all together. Maybe we can build this back again. But it won't happen in my time. It's too long a process.

SAM SILLARS: *The widower and his pigeons*

A widower, aged seventy-four, Sam lives on his own except for his budgie. The full shopping basket he has just brought back home with him indicates that he looks after himself properly. His council flat is decently maintained. Over the mantelpiece is a calendar bearing the inscription: 'Home is where we are treated best – and where we grumble most.'

Sam, however, is not a grumbler. Despite a tough life he remains a contented man. In the neighbourhood he is a favourite, because of the good turns he does. Lying on the sideboard, alongside the photograph of his wife, is an envelope containing a few shillings he is sending to the local Companionship Circle for the Elderly.

As a youngster I held a philosophy that simple things were the best. I still hold that philosophy today. Because they are the things that make life worth living – so you don't think it's worth while chasing moonbeams.

At the age of fourteen I left school. My job was in a glassworks. The job was hot and it was hard. The men were of a rough character, good in nature and heavy in their language. Nevertheless I enjoyed my job, till the war broke out on August 4, 1914.

Then, at the age of 16 years 11 months I enlisted on August 8th. I joined the King's Liverpools. I was imbued with the idea that I would be walking about in some immaculate style of military uniform. Instead, when we got to the barracks, the onrush of men was such, we slept on the floors. The food was short. For many days I walked around the streets of Liverpool still wearing my clogs, which I wore at home. Later things became a bit better.

I started to enjoy myself because I liked the army. Early in 1915 we was earmarked to go to France. I well remember the inspection that was made in the Waverley market. The Waverley market in Edinburgh had a gallery all around, and it was filled with Scottish citizens. The General's words ring in my mind today. He said, 'Remember this, boys, you're all going to France but you won't all come back.'

We landed at Le Havre. From there we went as far as we could go to the lines. Unfortunately for me – or fortunately if you like – the sergeant had it in for me. Finding me and one other in a comfortable farm outhouse he pointed his finger at me and said, 'You. Get out.' Two officers were put in our place. During the night a light shell hit this outhouse. Otherwise I wouldn't be here today. An instance of how fate plays funny tricks.

Up the line we went and the battle of Neuchatel started, on the tenth of March. We saw the hordes of German prisoners being brought in. We helped to shepherd them into places. We went up into the line. I was not to be there very long.

Along with three other men we took a chance to do something – which we was told to do, of course. And once again I must say I am lucky to be here – even if I did lose an eye. All four of us was hit. A sniper got me. He caught me on the left side of the head, close to the eye. If anybody would like to know what it feels like to be hit by a rifle bullet, from my experience I thought I had been hit by a Galloway boiler, it seemed that huge. Strange as it may seem, I was not knocked unconscious. I remember to this very moment getting on my knees and praying. And that German sniper, if I could meet him today I would shake him by the hand. I mean that. Because I am satisfied he knew that he had made me *hors de combat*. So he spared me.

I was dragged into the trenches. Again strangely enough I was able to walk as if there was nothing the matter with me, with the exception that I was blinded for a few weeks. This made me one of the lads who came home early. I had only seen a little bit of the carnage, compared with many who were there much longer. From what I saw I am convinced that war is the most terrible thing. I thought – and I still think – that men, intellectuals, should be able to organise people to go out and slay one another is terrible. I pray to God that no such thing is ever allowed to happen again.

I got back to my employment. The war ended. I was in work. I was married, and, happy with it. But later all the men who had been to the war was on the dole. I was one of them. It would appear that, instead of winning the war, we had lost it. We got 29 shillings on the dole. After a period of time you appeared before a Court of Referees and you was knocked off the dole for brief periods. I had a war pension and my wife was doing little part-time jobs. So that had to keep us. From then on it was a case of having to do what you could to get a job. I had certain principles which told me that, because of the job I had been doing, I had no right to do a labourer's job. I had been a skilled man. Machines had supplanted our way of making glass bottles.

I decided I had to do something and I took on a navvying job. It might sound a little bit out of plumb, but I must admit I didn't know the right end of a shovel. When I found myself alongside these navvy fellows I was completely lost. I was nearly heartbroken. I would have liked to have chucked the job, but I was thinking about what would have been said, 'He doesn't want work.' Which wasn't true.

And so – for a period – pick, shovel, barrow, etcetera, I carried on. I came out of work again. But that brief experience gave me confidence. I was able to find jobs that lasted for short periods that always gave me a chance of getting a stamp on my card.

Then, in 1924, I got a job for ten months working for the Council, working on the roads. In 1925 Mr Winston Churchill took us on the Gold Standard. And from being the recipient of nearly £4 a week our section dropped down to somewhere in the region of 54 shillings a week. What a drop! But it had to be accepted. If you wouldn't, there was plenty more to do the job.

We were living in a terrace house, a two-up, two-down. The lady I married had been a war widow, with a little family. A woman of quality, unsurpassed. I've lost her – to my regret. We got on very nice together. But there was times when friction arose through not being able to get a job. This was commonplace in every home. In particular a woman who did not understand the situation would ask her husband, 'How can *he* get a job when you can't?' That's what caused a little bit of unpleasantness from time to time.

Dismissal from one job made me more fortunate than the rest. From 1927 up to the year 1962 I had one employment, without a break, working on the highways as a labourer.

A year before the Second World War started I went into the ARP. We was detailed to do that. Till 1944 I was a full member of the Rescue Service. Like the rest of the boys I did my best. Sad nights. Glad nights.

The war ended, and back I went to my employment as a general labourer. I was pensioned off in 1962 and I believe I was treated right. In the interim before my retirement my wife met with a dreaded bad accident. With the result that we had to sleep downstairs. So onto the housing waiting list we went. That was in 1944. Thousands of others put their names on the housing list in that year. I was allocated a flat in 1953, nine years later.

Somewhere along the line I had a silent admirer, if I may say so. Whom he was I don't know. But after I had been allocated a flat I was called into the housing department manager's office. He told me that I had been recommended to do a little part-time job. It entailed me going around on a Tuesday night and a Thursday night, and if any lights needed replacing on the landings on these blocks of flats, it was my job to see to them. For that I got a little allowance off my rent.

As the flats filled up I was able to see that most of the tenants were very old people. So instead of keeping to the line of just going round on a Tuesday and Thursday night, I kept my eye on the lights every night. If I saw a light off I made it my business to see that no one got hurt. That was my primary thought, for the old people. Some of the old ladies were office cleaners. It meant that they had to be at work in the early hours of the morning, around six o'clock. To come down one, two, or three flights of steps in the dark was a risk. And also sometimes there were men found sleeping on the steps. So I saw that safety in that direction was going to be there for the old people.

All good things come to an end. My wife – God bless her – was failing. She passed away seven years ago, a year and a half after my retirement. This left me carrying out a last-minute order she gave to me on her deathbed. She asked me to look after myself. She didn't address me by my name. She said, 'Look after yourself, cock.'

In the lovely little flat I've got, which she had furnished with carpets etcetera, I have tried to maintain what she had asked me to do. We hear of people who are lonely. I don't question that for one moment. But fortunately for me I have my philosophy. If you want anything doing you've got to do it for yourself. My home is home – for anybody to come and view. And when I hear people say: 'You keep it very nice', that's an added tonic – I start doing a little bit more. Women are more capable when left on their own than what men are. I keep my home up-to-date as far as possible, but there's always that little bit you can't do. I suppose it's the feminine touch. Nevertheless – and I'm talking from the heart – I wish that every old man and woman was as comfortable as what I am. Some people are better off than myself. But they don't seem to have the know-how of living alone. Living alone means having to look after yourself, and promising yourself that you're not going to be dis-spirited because you have been left on a kind of a desert island. You're not on a desert island at all. You *are* on a desert island if you're only thinking in terms of yourself.

I have a hobby, which many people have not got. I walk a mile every day to my racing pigeons. On a fine day I'm able to sit, watch my birds, and get the pleasure out of them that only chaps like myself know how to get.

Apart from that I'm in the happy position to have been blessed with having thought for others. This has allowed me to concentrate

on disabled people when and where I can. All come alike to a
degree, but I'm in love with mentally handicapped children. These
children are the innocents of human society. We hear of flowers
that bloom and grow. To me mentally handicapped children are
something that grow, but they don't bloom. With the result that,
apart from what the children are losing, an added burden in the
way of a cross is inflicted on the shoulders of their parents. So, I
have to say, that mentally handicapped children, in fact mentally
handicapped people, are the Cinderellas of the invalid class. With
priority for mentally handicapped children, nobody has to come
to me twice for anything, be it a contribution or some kind of
physical help. All this has made me happy.

But the strange part about it is this. There are times when I
get a little down in the mouth over authoritarian, conceited,
people. While authority is able to condemn a man for keeping
pigeons or livestock of any nature, these people destroy, unwittingly,
the happiness of people. If only they gathered thought of how
they hurt a man's feelings when they say, with all the power they
hold, 'Thou shalt not keep this.'

I have had the misfortune to come in contact – or in combat,
should I say – with these people. My name is household in the
area where I live for my interest in pigeons. Little boys come to
me to ask for my guidance. I put them right, and on three or four
occasions, I regret to say, I have had the most trouble from people
I wouldn't have expected it from. These people believe in civil
rights; they believe in the rights of man. And to me civil rights and
the rights of man are my religion. I ask myself sometimes: are they
what they pretend to be?

On one occasion, with a batch of other men, I had to remove
our birds from one site to another. Through our battle we got the
second site. I had to go with a deputation and ask these people
why should they sentence me away from my hobby without being
given a chance to explain the nature of it. They wanted to remove
my birds because it was said they was a nuisance. What that
nuisance was I never knew. They were just listening to the stories
of people who had no idea of what a racing pigeon is.

Two prime factors about keeping racing pigeons are – and I've
kept them since I was twelve – they must be clean and healthy and
they mustn't loiter. For birds to loiter means time lost when racing. I still love pigeons and it's over my dead body that anyone

stops me from enjoying the pleasure. I've been along to various places and seen the interior of places where condemnation of my birds has come from. In one particular case of a man who had had so much to say, I wouldn't have allowed my pigeons to sleep in his house. Even to this day there's an undercurrent against the keeping of pigeons.

All I can say is: lucky is the man who has a hobby. If everybody had a hobby things would be different. Parents should realise that we're embroiled in vandalism, crime, what have you. People interested in pigeon fancying or livestock are born, not made. If any boy comes up to his Mam and his Dad and says, 'Mam, can I keep pigeons? Can I keep rabbits? Can I keep white mice?', then for God's sake let him have them. Because, whilst that boy is in the backyard enjoying his simple hobby of livestock, whatever it may be, his mother and his Dad knows where he is. And that's worth something. For once you stop the boy from having something that he likes you have broke his spirit.

Times are different from the dwelling point of view. Once, in the majority of backyards, the boy would have some kind of a hobby. But today we are living in flats. I live on my own. I would like a cat. I would like a dog. But that wouldn't be fair to other people who live in the flats. And so I'm prepared to accept that. (I have my budgie, but that doesn't make any difference.) A few weeks ago I heard about an MP speaking in the House of Commons about housing and council estates. This particular fellow's leanings are a long way from mine. But I have to say he was right. For he said that on too many occasions the pettifogging restrictions applied by local authorities were out of all reason.

On a council estate, with the help of the Royal National Homing Union, permission in hundreds of cases has been given for pigeon-cotes to be erected at a standard size, and all is working fine. Flats are a different cup of tea. Somewhere, somehow, space should be found by local authorities where people interested in livestock would be able to keep them. I walk a mile to mine, as I said. But some people are not happy about that. Somewhere down in London – the name has gone out of mind – a wonderful contribution was made by a housing estate. Allocated to each one or two blocks is a portion of land, and the people who rent this at a very low fee per year are able to keep livestock. Maybe a few head of poultry, it may be pigeons or rabbits or it may be that they only want to grow flowers. Nevertheless it's some kind of recreation. This is something that can be done by planning. But some folk are not so concerned with the little man.

I was once at a meeting where one of the principals there said that our pigeons and pigeon-cotes would, at a later date, be an eyesore to a building to be erected, when it was finished. I told him it was not, and I reminded him about a construction that had been allowed in the area that *was* an eyesore. He stopped short because planning permission had not been given to working lads in that instance. It had been given to a big shot, a name known all over the country. Why do some people who live far away from the things they object to, object as they do?

ADA GIBSON: *Satisfied customer*

Nearly sixty and unmarried, Ada looks after her widowed father. You enter their two-bedroomed flat on the seventh floor of a twelve-storey block from a silent, rubber-floored, corridor. Her father never goes out. She leaves him only to do the shopping. This is their world. The books, radio and TV set in the living-room are their links with life outside.

We left a two-bedroom house, which was rather damp, and came to live here, in this block of flats. We find it quite all right, in fact we like it very much. It's very nice to have a bathroom. The flat is clean. No backyard.

Some people come into flats with a prejudice against them even before they arrive. You should come with the idea that you are going to like it.

You can have fitted carpets here, but you couldn't have them in an old house. In fact you'd be wasting your money. For the walls and doors are warped, and you walk straight in off the street. The carpets wouldn't keep clean.

We have a lovely view here. There are the hills and we can also see the shopping precinct. It's easy for shopping. They've got all kinds of shops. You can do all your shopping there.

The neighbours like it. I've got two neighbours in the flats on this floor. They came at the same time as we did out of the same street. It's good to keep neighbours together, like that.

MAURICE LINDLEY: *The owner-occupier*

A young plumber working for himself. His small van stands on the path outside the suburban semi. It is seven o'clock on a Sunday evening. He has just returned from work, has had a bath, changed into clean clothes and is ready for the meal his wife is cooking for him on the gas-stove.

We talked it over before we got married. Though it was going to be a struggle we decided to buy a house right from the beginning. We got the house before we made the wedding date. I was living in my parents' corporation house in Wythenshawe on the south side of Manchester, and Dorothy was living with her parents in a terraced house opening right onto the street in Harpurhey, on the north side. We knew there was no chance of our getting a council house because of the long waiting list.

Nor did we want to pay £4, £5 or £6 a week to rent a flat and have nothing at the end of it. Dorothy's sister married and went into a rented flat. They struggled for six years before they could raise the £100 deposit that was required at that time. They had had three children meanwhile, so, on £11 a week wage, which was all he was getting, it was very hard to save for the house. We didn't want to start like that.

I'm twenty-seven, a plumber. I served my time. Until two years ago I worked for a firm. Then I started on my own. I was a little bit unhappy working for somebody else. So my wife and I agreed that it would be worth a try working for myself. So far it's not done too badly. It has been a struggle. It still is. I hadn't any capital – not a penny. I don't employ anyone. Most of your tools you already have. But when you need materials for a job there's a certain amount of money you have to lay out. And then there's the van.

We married four years ago and we've two kiddies. We had a lot of trouble getting the mortgage. We went to a few building societies, but not being a white collar worker they were a bit dubious about giving me a mortgage, although I was in a regular job. As far as the building trade worker is concerned, the building societies are just not interested. Because the work may be seasonal, I think. They would give us a mortgage, but not enough. On one terrace house we tried for, costing £2,500, they would give us only about fifty percent. We tried for another house in Partington that was about four years old at £2,900, and they wouldn't go anywhere near the mortgage we wanted, even though we didn't ask for a hundred percent. So we lost that house. My wife was working at the time, but they wouldn't take the wife's wage into consideration.

Then we went to an estate agent who was the agent for another building society and we got this house that way. It cost £3,250. It has three bedrooms and a bathroom. That's a 'break-through' partition which we can open up and turn the two rooms into one. We have put it in ourselves. And we've modernised the bathroom.

The mortgage was for eighty-five percent of the cost. It was from a different society and it helped that the estate agent was an agent for the society. We had to put £400 down. That was our savings. And we had to take an insurance policy out on an extra £200. We pay now £22.50 a month on the mortgage over twenty-five years. We pay a lot in rates. The rateable value is £94. We actually pay £95 in rates. It's just over a pound in the pound.

The surveyor's fee before you got the mortgage was about £8. Then there was another £12 surveyor's fee on completion. The solicitor's fee was £60, and we had the same solicitor as the people who owned the house, we found out. We thought it would have helped, but we still got a bill for £60.

We didn't have any hire purchase, except on the television. Most of the furniture had been given us. We bought a second-hand suite. Our parents gave us the money for the carpet.

It's not easy, but the only alternative would have been to live with one of our in-laws or go in a flat. We were determined to start with a house rather than get stuck. We might never have got out of it. We didn't want to pay out a fantastic rent for a flat and not be able to save.

We've got quite a long garden here. When we came out and saw the house and saw it was in a quiet avenue we saw it was ideal for children – even though we hadn't got any then. Dorothy was brought up in a terrace house and a street. As children you don't miss a garden, but as parents you know they're missing it. We wanted to give them some freedom in the garden and some grass. I think it has turned out as we wanted. I'm quite pleased.

It's not easy. We pay out £7 a week for mortgage and rates before we start. It depends on my getting orders. At this time of the year, in January, it's very slack. With two kiddies Dorothy had to stop work. Her wages are missing, obviously. She did manage to go back to work when we just had the one baby. She was working at a house, in a vet's surgery so she could take the baby with her. It was where she used to work before she got married. They took her back part-time. The surgery was at the front of the house and baby used to stay at the back. It was quite a good arrangement. She's always been fond of animals. We've got two cats now. We had a dog but it was a bit too playful for the children.

The interest to the building society has gone up three times, but on the last occasion they just extended the period of repayment. In January this year it dropped, so we are still repaying over twenty-five years.

There are disadvantages about being an owner-occupier if you're not a handyman and can't look after your own house. Fortunately, being a plumber, it's quite O.K. We've improved the house by putting in the 'break-through' doors. It was previously a brick wall separating the two rooms. We've changed the fire-place. It burns solid fuel. It used to be an open fire. And we've partly central-heated the house, and have a few radiators off it.

If you can't do it yourself, repairs and decorating cost a fantastic amount. If it's a rented house or a council house it's painted out-side for you, but you have to do your own if you are an owner-occupier. They are all owner-occupiers in this road, except for one rented house.

My income varies from week to week. It depends on the kind of job I've got on hand. If I'm doing, possibly, a central-heating job, I might be two weeks on end. One week I'm without wages, maybe two weeks without wages. Bills still have to be paid, unfortunately.

I think I can earn more than I could as an employed plumber. When I was working for somebody I was on the bare basic plumber's rate, and that wasn't sufficient. The rate has gone up since. I think it went up last July to £20 or £21 a week for forty hours. I never got any overtime. When I was working in that job I was only earning £16, as that was the plumber's rate then.

I put in longer hours now. If you were working on a job for somebody else you knock off at five o'clock. If it takes another hour to finish it you stay on and finish it.

We've had to go easy on spending. As regards holidays, fortunately my mother has got a caravan at Blackpool. Last year we had a week there. Sunny Blackpool. It was a terrible week we had. It was bad weather. It was August Bank Holiday week-end, so it only meant being a few days off work. The year before we managed to get away for a fortnight, camping with another couple in Cornwall. We bought a second-hand tent. We felt it when we came back. We felt we shouldn't have gone, we needed the money. I very rarely drink but I'm not over keen on it any way. We economise on food. We've not a lot of money to spend. We don't go buying expensive meat every day. We make do in the house, though we could do with new curtains. And the chairs need recovering. We did fairly well when the wife was working. We managed to get most of our things together: like the dining-room suite and the carpet. But since then we've had to borrow money. My wife's parents have been very good. We're not loaded with h.p. The only thing we've got on it is television. We did buy the dining-room suite on h.p., but we've paid that off now.

If you've got your own house you've always got something to sell. If you are really desperate you've got something there. You've not wasted your money. You've not spent it on the rent, and have nothing at the end of it.

We paid £3,250 for this house four years ago. Today these houses round here are fetching £4,000 to £4,500. They are very popular. It's very handy for town, and it's a quiet district. It can be a little too quiet. It suits us.

Mind you, over the twenty-five years you pay back more than double what you have borrowed. You pay back six or seven thousand on a three thousand loan. Possibly if you were to sell the house at that time you'd get that money back anyway.

The income tax relief on the mortgage interest does help, providing you are paying any tax at the top rate. At the moment I don't. I get relief for the two children. We are paying eight per cent on our mortgage. We could have got the option mortgage scheme reduction. At the time the option mortgage was considered, but it depends on how much income tax you are paying at the time. When we took the mortgage on I was on a pretty good wage so we got the relief through income tax.

I think we should be allowed to go back onto the option mortgage scheme. We were discussing it the other evening with an uncle who's just bought a house, and they've gone on to the option mortgage. They borrowed nearly a £1,000 more than we did and they are only paying £2 a month more. That's because of the option mortgage. You can change off it but you can't change onto it. I think that is it. In our case it would be an advantage if we could move onto it.

I can see why people want to buy council houses. If there were a surplus of council houses it would be all right. There will be more and more trying to get out of council houses with this fair rent thing.

But house prices have risen far too much. As I say, we'd probably get £4,000 for this house if we sold it today. They were built for £400 in 1928.

Don't think I've changed my views. I'm still a Labour man.

4. The professionals concerned

TIMOTHY TRENT *(Housing Manager)*
DR MCINTOSH *(General Practitioner)*
KENNETH GODWIN *(Teacher)*

TIMOTHY TRENT: *The management's view*

He is sixty, a housing official with responsibility for thousands of council houses and flats in a great Midlands industrial town. Though he is harassed by council tenants, by would-be council tenants, by councillors and by Ministry officials, he manages to retain his composure and, on certain projects, even his enthusiasm. His phone is probably the busiest of any official in the Corporation. Graphs showing monthly progress cover the walls of his office. But years of experience have taught him ways of circumventing red tape. Sitting at his desk he may sometimes look and talk like a bureaucrat, but you feel there is a human being inside the neat grey suit.

Housing management doesn't just mean giving tenants the key of a house, collecting the rent and leaving it at that. We see management in a much wider sense. It's our job to assist those who want problems solved, if they wish us to. Also to see they maintain a decent living condition inside the house, along the lines laid down in the rent book.

On the other side you have thousands of families living in need in other parts of the area, and it's my job to try and rehouse them. The main demand comes from a huge slum clearance programme. We ask them to make at least three choices of where they would like to live. We don't 'decant'. That means we don't transfer them all into one fixed area. We give them a right to choose. There is a difficulty here, for some areas are more popular than others. But we've achieved quite a high degree of success in placing people where they want to go.

People don't like going a long way out. Travelling seems to be the biggest problem. The fares are astronomical. I've talked to my letting staff about how to deal sympathetically with new tenants.

For them it's a meteoric step. They are living in the clouds. If you're not careful half the things you tell them are going in at one ear and out at the other. They're so excited, their minds are filled by just one fact: 'Look, we're moving.' We try to be as kindly as possible, and also explain the responsibilities they now have, such as keeping the house clean and the gardens tidy, and paying the rent in the method we now use. They come to us to pay the rent instead of having collectors though it has its obvious problems.

If I was given the chance I would like to have more staff on the estate side, looking after welfare. I would like to get them into every one of our houses at least once every twelve months, even if it was only to meet the people and say, 'Good morning.' Sometimes tenants do things which are against the regulations. For instance, they may move the cooker to a new spot or they may change the electrical wiring. This may look nice, but it can be dangerous.

About tenants painting the outsides of the houses, we are against this. It's not that we object to having different colours. It's that some people have very different standards of doing it. And when you come to other kinds of exterior work, such as boundary fencing, if you allow people to do this it's beautiful if a chap has plenty of money and he puts up a lovely fence. But next door a fellow is putting up orange boxes. Before you know where you are you've got a slum. We'll give people permission to do things, but we want to know what's going on.

We had a case where someone had taken all the doors out and put beautiful glass doors in, without our permission. The house changed hands. The new tenants found that the doors didn't fit properly. Because the previous tenant had done it, it was our responsibility to put them right.

We permit four-legged pets in the houses but not in the multi-storey flats – for an obvious reason. As for pigeons, I don't really think it's practicable to have pigeon-cotes for children on the estates. Unless they are properly looked after they will be abused. The pigeon racing enthusiasts are different. They will see that their birds are well looked after. We permit them under rigid controls.

We've got two blocks of multi-storey flats with children's adventure playgrounds, with all kinds of built-in circles and humps. But the ludicrous position is that nobody uses them, for the simple reason that there are no children in those blocks any longer. It's

3

a rigid policy on our estates that we are taking all children under fourteen out of multi-storey accommodation. In no circumstances are we putting new families with children under that age into tower blocks. Previously our policy was that no family could get a house unless they had a child under nine. But recently we've had this change of policy. It's a major step forward. The new policy helps those who want houses – and they mostly do. It also helps to relieve a shortage of flats.

If they build any more flats they are going to be low rise up to three or four storeys. At last we are building in the centre of the city, which just lay waste after the demolition, instead of trying to get people to move outwards. They just don't want it. They've lived all their lives in the city, and they want to stay there.

The rents for our houses vary between £3.80 and £4.40, inclusive of rates. Those are the older, pre-war type. Flats are not necessarily cheaper than houses. Two-bedroom flats can be anything up to £4.50. When the 'Fair deal for housing' comes into operation I just don't know what's going to happen to those rents.

When I have young people for training I always say to them, 'Before you make an absolute decision to go into housing there's one paramount question you must decide: do you want to work with people and for people? Or do you want to be quite aloof from them, as in accountancy?' As a housing official it's your duty and your pleasure to try to help people along. It's not just rehousing people; it's seeing that those people are happy and contented in their houses. The provision of four walls is not a home.

And now I'm on my pet subject – the old folk. If you take them away from their Bingo, their church and their friends you are starting a new housing problem. This is important. We are going to be faced with a growing number of Senior Citizens. Within one of our areas we have had an outstanding success. This is one of my babies. I say this with the greatest of enthusiasm. Sooner or later you are going to have on most estates a great number of old people who have brought their families up and who have now been left alone. I have round here only too many three-bedroom houses, with man or wife, or generally a woman on her own of advanced age, dearly wanting smaller accommodation because they can't look after larger houses. But at the same time they come to you and say, 'Look, Mr Trent, I don't want to move from this district.'

What can you do within the confines of that particular district?

It's too late to try and make amends afterwards. They do something very successfully in Norway. And we've seen it done here now. It's this. You decide in an estate of, say, 3,000 houses, you should have a block of flats or bed-sitters, what are called 'warden controlled'. We've got one block of forty-one flats, thirty of them bed-sitters, ten one-bedroom flats and a two-bedroom flat for a warden.

What happens here is this. These flats are let at a very reasonable rent. More ladies live to an old age than men. So you find that the ladies are quite content to take bed-sitters. The ten one-bedroom flats are let to man and wife. The warden's job is not to nurse them in any way, for these flats are quite self-contained. They have their own front door. If a person wants to keep himself to himself he's perfectly entitled to do so. But nevertheless the loneliness, which is of paramount importance amongst old people, is completely eradicated. I went to one block where I knew the people formerly. Loneliness had really been putting years on them. We put them in this place. We pointed out to them they were so designed that there was a bell push or a bell string, which came down to the floor, in every room, so that even if they fell, whether in kitchen, hall, bedroom or landing, they could just pull this bell and the warden would be there immediately. So the sense of fear of being caught ill, without being able to warn anybody, was eradicated.

Every morning the warden would say: 'Well, I'd like you to come down to the common-room for a cup of coffee.' It's a cosy room with armchairs and a big television. It's quite voluntary, but they all come. The idea of this is that she then sees they are all right, without having to knock on their doors, as if she were intruding. When I went there it was a joy to see the years that had been taken off these people. I found half a dozen of the men, revolutionaries, changing the world, in one corner. The ladies were in another, talking with pride about their grandchildren.

Psychologically, these people realised that somebody cared. This is the important thing. The joy that came out of the faces of those people. I'll never forget it. I would see that on every estate there is some warden-controlled property. Not to be filled with people from everywhere in the city. But when someone has brought a family up and done their duty as a citizen they have a right to accommodation which gives them comfort, within the area where they used to live. They could still go to their church or Bingo.

If they have this to look forward to, believe me they will go through life far more contented than they do at the moment. Without it people going to be rehoused in the centre are scared stiff with fears and worries about things that are going to face them.

The old age pensioner. It's a pet with me. When planning takes place it must provide for old people to have warden-controlled homes in the area where they live.

In spite of all the set-backs you get in this job it's a joy when you can see somebody who has been made happy by something you have done. I remember one dear old soul who came in to see me. I think she knew we couldn't provide what she hoped for. She said: 'Mr Trent you haven't been able to give me what I wanted, but it's been very nice talking to you.' That was a compliment that meant an awful lot to me.

DR MCINTOSH: *Some remarkable recoveries*

Although it is forty years since he left Glasgow he has not lost his Scots accent. He likes his job as a general practitioner, which takes him inside a great number of slum homes and also into many new council flats. So he is well placed to assess the 'before' and 'after' effects. Dr McIntosh is now well off himself. His son is training to be a doctor at a famous London hospital, his daughter is at a university, and his wife is active in social work.

I was brought up in a tenement in Glasgow. It was a very poverty-stricken place, and a place I was determined, even as a small boy, to get out of. The only way I could see of getting out of it was by having a very good education. When I was a boy I had to go to hospital and the specialist diagnosed that there wasn't very much wrong. But I was so impressed by his kindness and with the hospital set-up that I went visiting several places as far as I could as a youngster – I couldn't get inside the wards or anything – and I gradually made up my mind that I was going to be a doctor. I was almost scorned by my neighbours and my pals, who said, 'Look who's going to become a doctor', sort of thing. Because we were brought up in such a slummy kind of atmosphere that even the idea of getting out of it had been lost. They had lost all hope of doing anything except sticking in these places.

Eventually I did qualify. In those days there were no grants. So you had to work if your parents couldn't afford to keep you, while you were a student. And you had to do this not only in your holiday time but also in your spare time while you were at the university. I thoroughly enjoyed my time at Glasgow University. I thought it provided a good training. I couldn't ever dream of specialising. This was just because I couldn't afford it. The moment I qualified I had to get a job.

My first job was in South Wales. I got some very good training there too. And there I saw how the poor people in that area lived – and particularly the miners. I only once went down a mine and I hope never to go down a mine again. When I did go down it was to see a man who was dead. From there I went to the Black Country and I worked eighteen months there, near Cradley Heath, where the main occupation was making chains. They did it in the backs of their own houses. They had their own little forges, and a lot of them used to brew their own beer, since they used to sweat a lot at their work. We got plenty of lead poisoning, because the vats they had were lead lined, and they used to drink the dregs. That was my first experience of meeting people who had lead poisoning from beer drinking!

The next move was to Manchester where I bought the practice by a series of machinations, for I had exactly £100 saved up. I had to buy the practice and the house. In those days you had to buy a practice. I managed to raise the money on loan. That was nearly forty years ago.

In those days the worker was on the panel and the wife and children were private patients. The poorer people used to pay a collector about sixpence a week or something like that. And of course you gave them medicine as well for the sixpence a week. In those days it was really very tough indeed on the worker. If he didn't work for a considerable time he then ran out of benefit as regards his doctor, and he would no longer have a doctor either. He was knocked off the panel.

I came to work here. At that time it was mainly a working-class practice. At that time there was tremendous unemployment as well. Though I loved my work, I hated book-keeping and clerking.

I used to send out my bills once a year. The result was that quite a lot of people had shifted and other people had forgotten that I had ever gone to them.

The kind of work you did then was rather different from what it is today. You didn't have as many patients, so you had time to talk to the people, to get to know their personal problems, to know the families well. They looked on you not just as a doctor who gave them medicines for their illnesses, but as a sort of Father Confessor and as a person who would help them with their worries. They had warm feeling towards the doctor. This was the kind of relationship which was established in those days. It could be established today, too, if the doctor had time. It is this lack of time which is losing the GP his personal touch with patients.

Without a doubt housing has a big effect on the health of patients. First of all, in addition to poverty, which leads to under-nourishment of course, the mere fact that these people were hard up led to over-crowding. In these slum houses you could be almost certain that any infection which came into the house spread right through the family. You would always have three or four cases instead of one case when you went there.

You would get a kind of hopelessness, especially on the part of the wife. She had all this to contend with; she never finished cleaning – cleaning the children and the house, trying to make a meal and make her money go as far as possible. She got prematurely old, dull and hopeless. She felt that, if it wasn't for the children, she could do without living altogether. This was the quite frequent attitude among very poor houses. Others if they didn't have that extent of poverty, and the houses were better, didn't have that same extent of illness. There's no question that illness was much greater in the poorer households. This is natural.

In the old days we used to have things like whooping cough. Whooping cough is a dreadful thing. You don't see nearly so much of it today. If one child got it you had the whole lot getting it. Every time they coughed they were sick, they vomited. You had this to contend with in a house with three or four children, sometimes more. If any infection came along, such as measles, you got an epidemic in these poorer areas.

Earlier we also had the odd case of polio. We got panic stricken if polio occurred in one of the over-crowded houses. There's quite an incubation period and we were frightened that the rest of them were going to get polio. Then there is any throat infection, which was quickly carried to the rest of the family. Concurrently there were those gastro-enteritis infections, diarrhoea, dysentery and so on. I did some research into this with the encouragement of the Professor of Bacteriology at the university. We were quite amazed at the number of dysenteries we discovered, which we never expected to occur in general practice. We took it all as being food poisoning. But it's not true. They are germ infections, and ones that one gets from the other, because of their close contiguity. This was almost endemic in some of the poverty-stricken parts. We get that today – but not to the same extent.

Today bad housing conditions lead to a lot of the respiratory diseases, because they are close on top of one another and if one child gets a respiratory infection it goes right through. You get bronchitics. Among young children you get them constantly coming to you with colds. The mother despairs and says, 'No sooner is he getting better from one than he is having another.'

Bronchitis can be disabling. The first time it doesn't matter: they get better. Then they get another attack and they get better. But ultimately it can create such a bad condition of the lungs and such difficulty in breathing that it becomes disabling. Your chronic bronchitic is already a man who can't cope with his work as well as he should do. In the winter time there are some patients of mine who can't go to work at all. Or if they go to work they get a cold – and that's them settled. We have a large number of chronic bronchitics here.

It's generally thought that dampness in the home could have something to do with the high number of people suffering from arthritis but I don't think we have anything like 100 per cent scientific proof on this. But rheumatics always complain that when the weather's damp they are a lot worse, or that they know when the damp weather's going to come on, that they are kind of weather vanes.

When people are rehoused there are good reactions and bad reactions. From the health point of view rehousing is phenomenal in that it absolutely makes a difference to them. It's quite amazing. Let me explain how we know this. We know that Mrs A., who has lived in a slum house, with, say, four children, and poor conditions, sends for me very frequently. She gets rehoused in my own area. I then see her in her new flat with the heating and everything else and I find that my attendances on that family are not one fifth of what they were before. This is a fact.

The psychological difference it can make is also phenomenal. I went to a family once that I though were the most slovenly, decrepit, family I had ever been to. The mother couldn't care less whether the children had clean clothes or dirty clothes or whether the children were even fed. They lived in a real squalid little place. This woman was rehoused in one of the council flats. I was called there and the difference was amazing. From being a real frowzy, bedraggled person, she was neat and clean and tidy. So was the house. And so were the children. The place had an atmosphere of optimism about it. She had something to live for. No longer was she the down-and-out I thought she was. I thought she could never recover from that condition, but she did – and very rapidly. And that surprised me. So much so that I even told my wife about it – although I didn't tell her who the patient was. That was really quite something. I have a number of such cases but she was really so down-and-out I had to comment on it. I just didn't believe my eyes when I saw her in her new home. She was a completely different person, with a completely different family.

As regards the disadvantages, the one thing I would urge on Councils, when they rehouse people, is for someone to go and meet the people and get to know them for a little while before they rehouse them. They should find out about their families and their friends because, when rehousing people, they should remember they have their roots, their friends and their families. Try not to split these people up, if you can avoid it. Try to send them all on the same housing estate or within easy reach of each other, especially families. For example, in the Collegiate area, which has been knocked down, I thought it was marvellous that they were all going to wonderful new flats, until one of my patients came up to me who was crying bitterly. I asked her what it was all about. 'Well,' she said, 'they're sending my mother there and they're sending me and my kids somewhere else five miles away, and the other daughter is going somewhere else. We're all being split up.'

This is not the only case. You get a number of cases in these small streets where the mother – or the grandmother I should say – is the centre. She is the matriarch of the family. They all come to her with their difficulties. The married daughter is perhaps two doors away or across the road. And they have got *their* children.

Any difficulties or illnesses with the grandchildren and they all come to the grandmother. They are a closely knit family – as families should be. They all help each other. The prospect of being split up appalled them, even though they all knew they were going to nicer houses. They wanted the nice flats but they wanted to be together. Surely the Council, in rehousing, should make some effort to understand these things and not spoil a very benevolent action by forgetting the human factors. This is really terribly important. If their family had been kept together they would have been in the height of heaven with the new surroundings. But being split, the new flats did not compensate. Families must not be treated just as a number on the roll.

Then there is the psychological problem of those going to new flats. This is particularly true of people living on their own, or even an old couple. Particularly if they are living way up they have a feeling they are cut away from everybody. Individuals vary as to their reaction to this. The older you get the more difficult it is to make friends. As a youngster you make friends, and you grow up with your friends. As you grow older you rely more on your friends because you are not chasing or finding new ones. Now if you get transferred to a flat perhaps eight storeys high and you get separated from your friends it makes things a little more difficult. You find it hard to make up to your new neighbours. They may be young people who don't have much time for old people. So you have these problems. I think you'll always have them as long as you have flats up ten floors or more. It's easier to overcome them if everything is on the ground. Then people can sit outside and say 'Good morning' to their neighbours. In fact there is one woman my wife knows who is so lonely in this flat that she keeps her door open in order to hear the sounds of other people.

Though there is a small minority who couldn't care less, most poor people want to live in decent homes. Their ambition is not to get rich or to do anything to the detriment of their fellow creatures. For the vast majority their ambition is to live an honest, decent, life, but to have a reasonable amount of comfort round them, for themselves and their children. It should not be too much to ask of society to help them to do that.

KENNETH GODWIN: *A teacher and his children*

About himself and his profession he says, 'Just as miners are prone to get silicosis, we get the disease of talking at people rather than to them. When you've been in it as long as I have you can't get out of the habit.' His wife is also a school teacher, and they have two very bright children of school age. Although they live in a pleasant suburb he knows a great deal about bad housing in the congested cotton town where he works, for he has become closely involved in the lives of his pupils, both in and out of school.

I was born in this city forty-three years ago. I suppose I've been unadventuresome, as the only time I have lived away was when I was in the Forces and at college. I rather like what I'm doing and you can see a certain amount of reward. Also in our area you are accepted after a time far more easily than you would be in a different social type of area. Once you have convinced our kids and our parents that you are well intentioned towards them – even if they think you have some peculiar views – you do get co-operation from most of them.

There is a great loyalty between parents and the children, and, no matter how poor the conditions may be, I am always against putting kids in care of the local authority unless there is absolutely no alternative, because sometimes we who have had greater advantages seem to think there is only one kind of system under which a child can be happy.

I've taught in the area for nearly seventeen years and I've been headmaster of this school for seven. It is a school which has every kind of disadvantage. It's not old enough to be of interest to people like Betjeman, but it's old enough to have every disadvantage. For example, all the space is high, instead of being where the kids can use it. It's fifteen or twenty feet up. So that's bad for heating, spacing and display. It should have been pulled down a long time ago. When it was built in 1884 I suppose it served its purpose.

The parents come to us with problems that are not strictly educational. It's like a game of kidology. They know and I know that it's not really the problem of dinner tickets or gangs on the children's way home that they have come to see me about. You go through the motions of discussing the supposed topic and then you get down to what's really worrying them. When you have gained a working relationship with parents in many cases you are able to do something useful, or put them in touch with some Council department which can. And this is what I like to think we are doing.

Most of the houses round here were built seventy years ago. They weren't built for the purpose which most folks wish to use them for today. If you were working a 16½-hour day or more, when you came home you ate, you flopped exhausted into bed, and woke up in time to go to work the next day. All you needed was what you could call a 'roofed bed' for a house. On Sunday you made up your rest or you went out. Now that working hours have shortened and leisure has increased these houses have become insufficient for the need.

This new wish for a better home affects people according to their age. The folk who are least affected are the older people, who have known very little difference and who are willing to put up with it. The next generation are relatively satisfied, again because they have known no difference. They go out to Bingo or clubs, or they put flying ducks across the wallpaper or paper the ceiling in a different way, trying to improve what they can.

The folk who find it most irritating are the young ones, the under-thirties, who are less prepared to accept previous conditions, and who either spend as much time away as they can or show their frustrations in other ways. If they have friends living in different conditions they are loath to invite them back to their own homes. Consequently they tend to make their friends in similar groupings. If one of them 'breaks away', for example goes to work and lives temporarily somewhere else, the discontent grows when he returns. He grows increasingly impatient with those who are prepared to put up with things as they are. That is a most encouraging thing in my view. If these people get organised as the consumer or environment groups are doing, then God help the people who are mucking them about. The criterion of success in this area, unfortunately, is to get out. This denudes the area of natural leaders. We have very few resident professional people and only two resident councillors in this ward.

I'm thinking of a boy and girl I knew round here who got married. They made their old house as nice as they could. They didn't want to start a family right away, because they hoped to move out to a more salubrious area. This didn't work out. A baby came, which meant, of course, that the girl couldn't work. So the income was very much reduced. Another child followed. The husband wasn't able to raise the amount of cash needed for a deposit on a house. Being doomed to remain in the area, their whole attitude to life altered. They have not had so enjoyable a life as they had planned. I'm pretty sure that, now this lad has gone back to a hard drinking circle of men of his own age, more trouble will start.

The teenagers are the objects of a rather unfair advertising campaign: 'Don't repair, replace.' Some of them in unskilled jobs earn a reasonable amount of money to start with. But when they reach eighteen and want a man's wage they are chucked out, and another fifteen year old is brought in. The young man feels bloody about it, particularly if things aren't too good at home. He get's no satisfaction from his job. And because of the conditions of his home he can get no satisfaction there.

The children are in the home far longer than the parents who go out to work. They have less resistance to the bad qualities of the housing: insufficient heating and lighting, dampness and lack of hygiene. There are some children who are eneuretic, who, when they can go to a nice warm toilet inside their new flat without having to go across the cold yard, immediately cease to be bed-wetters. This sometimes amazes people who should know better.

Similarly we found at school that when we got indoor toilets, some of the girls who had advanced early and had started men-struation, who had previously had nervous distress about using the toilets, lost it when they could lock the toilet doors.

The kiddies at our school, because they are usually the youngest element in the family, get last turn at whatever facilities there are. This applies, first of all, to sleeping places. The older children have the better sleeping place. If you are overcrowded and you are sleeping sex-wise – that means all females together and all males together – you cannot get to sleep if you are a younger one until the older one has arrived home. Even if you are asleep, the odds are that you are disturbed.

I can think of five homes where, apart from this, the children can't get a good night's sleep whenever it rains, because they are shifting beds or having to go and sleep downstairs. They give up the fight of trying to keep the upper storey dry. I know places where the cooker is left on all night with the door open so that you may get a bit of warmth coming in that way.

The same thing will hold for washing. If the mother has only one washing container and leaves the breakfast things in the sink before going out to work and the child hasn't by then had a wash or even a swill, he's not going to take it over pots. So he comes to school with his eyes bunged up with sleep. Obviously cleaning his teeth is a very fond hope. And although the launderettes have improved things to some extent, the drying of nappies and other clothes is a big problem.

If one of the children has an illness you cannot isolate, convalesce or recuperate if you are on top of one another.

These constant pressures do encourage nervousness, bad temper, insomnia and all sorts of pressure manifestations, which show themselves in anti-social behaviour.

According to the Medical Officer's report the rate for bronchitis in this district is three times as high as it is in the residential suburbs of the city. The children are in these houses for most of the day and night. It has a cumulative effect.

Another great disadvantage is the lack of privacy. There isn't any. It has a big effect on reading and homework and study. I was very pleased when the local library put a room at the disposal of children who were preparing for certain schools exams. I think the school authorities should make a room available to all children who want quiet to do their homework.

There is a strict hierarchy in the family rules. The younger you are the less place you have in the hierarchy. The 'ideal' school-child who is quiet and polite would be just walked into the carpet in an overcrowded house.

I think all children want space. If you have no space or privacy things get broken, people tread on toys. It leads to conflict. If you want to do something maybe your sister wants to do something else, and that's tricky if there's only a limited space. When it comes to physical activity for these children they are rather like puppies. They just want to run about. When we take our very small ones out to a park the pattern is, first, ten minutes of utter exhaustion. Then you sit down. Only after that can you organise something as a group. There is boundless energy, but it isn't stamina energy. They very soon get exhausted and the number who sleep in the transport coming back is a big one.

We all hear about gangs taking over when space is set aside for children. This is because these young people have never had a training in the use of space.

Generally speaking re-housing round here is successful, particularly if people have moved into low-rise housing. The difficulties come in these high-rise flats. They are all right for people who are mobile or who haven't young children. If you have very young children in high-rise flats, as has been shown in Leeds and Bristol and elsewhere, they feel just as restricted as they would in their old houses, perhaps more so. Because at least you could let them – with their older brothers or sisters – play in the street, where they would be within call or grab. You could rush out and grab a child if you heard any shrieking. But if it's shrieking sixteen floors down, you can't. We have kiddies coming into our nursery who just can't communicate.

For the first week or so they just sit in a corner. They are not developed. The very young and the very old are the ones who find moving into new property the most difficult.

Another thing is that it does break up this social unity, the neighbourliness of life. The material difficulties are solved but new social difficulties arise.

The position of the grandmothers is something noteworthy in our kind of area. The grans are the source of experience; they look after the grandchildren; they still have a lot to give to the younger people. These old girls were brought up with very firm ideas: neatness in handwriting, never living beyond your means, personal standards of cleanliness, knitting, brownstoning your step, rinsing the milk bottles . . . Once the grans are on your side you can't put a foot wrong. It's a sort of matriarchy. It's nice to know they have their place. But in slum clearance they lose it. And then they go under.

5. High, damp and mouldy

ERNEST DOVE · PHYLLIS SIMONS · DORIS MASON · THOMAS
JONES *(Architect)* · GRAHAM STODDARD *(Child Care Officer)*

ERNEST DOVE: *New flats – green mould*

*Ernest Dove, fifty, lives with his wife and eighteen year old son on the
fourteenth floor of a block of council flats. He was employed as a 'Faulty
Ales Supervisor' for a brewery, dealing with complaints by pubs, but
three years ago he was required by the hospital to stop working because
of his chronic bronchitis and heart trouble. Until then they had lived for
thirteen years in a two-up, two-down, but, because they were on top
priority for health grounds, were granted a council flat with relatively
little delay.*

My trouble started when I was forty-eight when I had this sudden
collapse. I had to give up work on hospital advice, and I found out
later it was a heart condition plus chronic bronchitis. My wife
also suffers from very bad arthritis, and is having hospital treatment. The Health Department decided we should move from where
we lived. It was in a slum area but not due for demolition. They
did a wonderful job in getting us moved so quickly.

We were offered quite a few tenancies by the Corporation in
flats. But the condition of them was filthy, absolutely disgraceful.
Then we were offered the flat where we now are, and it was a
really clean flat. It had been built about two years. It was a top
floor, 14th storey flat, but we were so desperate to get somewhere
where our health might improve that we accepted it.

We went in in May 1970, and all seemed to go well until September when a sudden deterioration set in. We began getting damp
in the flat and after a few weeks a green fungus began to appear
on the furniture and the bedding. I had a carpet which went completely green-mouldy. Just imagine going into a bedroom where
you've got a carpet with green mould. The smell was intolerable
at times. There have been nights when we have brought the mattress

off the bed and slept on the floor in the living-room. There was fungus on the walls and ceilings and it contaminated our furniture, carpets and bedding. It affected our clothing too, my shoes in particular. I had three pairs at the time, a really good pair I used to save for week-ends and two pairs I used for knocking about in. I always kept a good shine on my shoes. I went to get my best pair after laying them aside for two days and they were absolutely covered with green mould.

We got an inspector to come down from the Housing Department and he had some meters which measured dampness. He put these on our bed and told us it was damp. He tested the walls with another device and stated that the walls were in a very bad condition. You daren't put clothing in the bedroom. You got a dark green, horrible fungus. It was like something from the slums years and years ago. Some of these flats they are building today will deteriorate to the same condition within a few years.

They say to us that this condensation is just due to our neglect in not having windows open. This is an absolute fallacy, for I can't sleep with my windows shut, summer or winter. To keep the damp down it became necessary for us to have electric fires going in the bedrooms and living-room, plus the underfloor heating. The expense of it was terrific. I'm on social security. That covers the rent but it doesn't cover heating and lighting. I imagine a flat lower down the block has to put four shillings a day in the meter. Last winter we had to put ten shillings a day into it. We had to curb that; we didn't put the electric fire on till five o'clock in the evening to save expense. If we had put it on any earlier we just wouldn't have been able to cope with the bills.

All the neighbours on this top floor have had the same trouble. They have had it in other multi-storey blocks too. I have seen the flat next-door and the bedroom, in particular, was in an appalling condition. In the flat across the passage the son found that his clothing in the wardrobe had been contaminated with this fungus. So the mother took the clothing down to the housing authorities, but they just didn't want to know. They said there was nothing they could do about it. Her intention was to claim damages, but they said they could do nothing in that respect, though they would try to do something about stopping the fungus. We've had to throw things away ourselves: a carpet and blankets. I'm an ex-serviceman and so an Old Comrades Association bought a blanket for me and bedding, as we just hadn't the money.

After those men came with the damp measuring clock a workman visited us and said, 'I've come to decorate the flat.' I said, 'That's a bit unusual. It was done only a few months ago.' He said, 'It's over this fungus. I've got to paint it.' Actually it was only a treatment to the fungus that he was going to do. What he wanted to do was to strip off parts of the wallpaper where the fungus was and put patches here and patches there. That was all he wanted to do. Our rooms are nicely decorated and to do this would have been a crime. So he did whole walls and ceilings. And we couldn't decorate it afterwards because this stuff he was using – a very expensive product – doesn't allow papering or painting on top of it. It's said it will eventually kill this fungus and whatever it's coming from, though that's still got to be proved.

It's two or three months since they did it and it's getting towards the winter. By then we should be able to judge the effects of this stuff. When they first wanted to give the flat this treatment I refused on the grounds that it would desecrate the place. They have made a reasonable job of the bedroom.

Then there's the lifts. When I was moved the housing visitor knew I was being rehoused on health grounds. They offered us a multi-storey flat. We said we'd prefer a house on overspill.

They said that that would take years, there were that many on the waiting list. So we said, 'Right, we'll just have to take what we can get.' We took the flat knowing it was on the top storey. But at the time I wasn't fully aware of my condition. Then one of the lifts went out of action for three months. Therefore the odd and even floors were using the other lift. It was in a terrible state of disrepair. On several occasions I've had to walk up twenty-eight flights of stairs and I've been in a total state of collapse. My doctor has been informed about this and about the smell in the bedroom. He's advised us that we should get out before this next winter. He has given us a further note for the Health Department and we are waiting the outcome of this.

Apparently the people who erected these lifts went into liquidation and now another firm, the Express Lift Company, has taken them over and has got them into a serviceable condition.

It's not right for anyone like an old person or someone suffering from a heart complaint or shortage of breath. And I'm not alone on this floor in that way. My married daughter came one lunchtime and she was trapped in a lift for over half an hour. She became hysterical. It got her to that state her nerve had completely gone. She couldn't go back to work that afternoon. And to this day she will not go in a lift alone. It's a terrible sensation to be locked in a lift. I've been locked in it several times myself. I know someone will come sooner or later, but not everybody realises that. My daughter still comes here two or three times a week and she walks up. She's only a young girl – twenty-two – but even so it's wrong.

You can't blame the children all the time for the lifts going wrong. At the present time these flats are in a very clean state. When we first came here the corridors and staircases used to be in a terrible condition. The lifts were fouled at times – more so at weekends, with drunks. They used to say it was kids, but anyone with any sense would know if it was adults that had relieved themselves.

At first we quite liked the flats. There's a splendid view from the top floor. We don't mind the height – we have got used to it. Even in winter you can see for miles. It's all lit up. It was summer when we came and had the veranda open. I enjoyed having the bath, the hot water system and the inside toilet – not having to go outside at night to relieve yourself. You just go out of your bedroom and into the toilet.

It was the sudden deterioration last September. The place became like an iceberg. It's much colder on the top floor. I have another married daughter on the sixth floor in this block. It's lovely and warm there. She can do without the underfloor heating. Then there was this fungus trouble and the smell. I used to dread going to bed. As I said, we have slept on the floor in the next room and that's what we intend to do again if we're still here this winter.

I think it's all wrong that young children should live in flats. We know they have to have somewhere to live, but they shouldn't be put in these flats. People complain about the children because they make a noise. They do make a noise. But they have got to live, they have got to play. On a wet day they have nowhere to play, so they play in the lifts and in the corridors. If they were in a house they could play inside their own home, without disturbing other people. The sound in these flats is ridiculous. If you speak in a loud tone of voice the people in the next flats can hear you and you can hear them.

There are quite a few little playgrounds for the children when it's fine, and they do play there. There's a little grass verge here too, but they get chased off it if they play there. They have erected a fence along the riverside, but it's inadequate and the children are just climbing over.

We hope eventually to get to overspill, about nine or ten miles away. My sister's little boy was very seriously ill with bronchial asthma whilst he was living in the town. He's been removed for quite a few years now and he's free of it. I'd like to settle down there. My chances of an exchange are remote for I've been trying for a long time to get there.

Compared with my previous rent this rent is absolutely ridiculous. Fortunately I've got a son, aged 18, living with me. Without that lad I would have nothing. My rent is £4.01 a week, but I am subsidised with social security. Yet without that lad I still couldn't afford to live here. My rent in Cambridge Street was thirty-one shillings a week. We were without hot water and a bath, but we didn't have this discomfort of cold and damp.

These multi-storey flats have some good things about them, but if they had spent more care in planning them they would have been better.

PHYLLIS SIMONS: *Children on the 14th floor*

Mrs Phyllis Simons, small, blonde, bespectacled, lives with her lorry driver husband and eleven year old son on the 14th floor of the same block of council flats. They both go out to work and return home at about the same time. As we talked the boy made us all cups of tea.

I first came here two years ago, and when we first arrived I really liked it. I hadn't worked for ten years and I liked it so much I never budged out. Then the winter came and the bedrooms became wringing wet and it was freezing. I reported this to the Housing but got no satisfaction. All they came to do was the veranda. The rain lodged in it because there was no way of draining it.

Then the men came and stripped all the ceiling in my bedroom and painted it and painted two walls. They said this special paint was supposed to hold the mould. I don't believe it will. I'll wait for the winter now to see. This is still an experiment. If some of those fellows from the Housing would come and live here for a month in the winter I'd move out to let them. It's absolutely freezing. I've got to have the heating on eighty and then I have to turn the electric fire on as soon as I get home from work. In any floor below the top you don't have to have the heating because those flats are warm enough.

Then there's the difficulty with children in these flats. The boy is eleven. He's a nice, helpful boy, he does all the errands. I have to go out to work now to cover the rent, it's over £4. When I come home and send him errands neighbours shout at him, 'Stop playing in the lift'. He can't play. He takes a ball downstairs and they say, 'Shift the ball'. If they are near the rubbish chute room and it starts smoking they say the kids have set it on fire. Sometimes grown-ups send things down the chute which are hot and that sets it on fire. There's nowhere for these lads of eleven and upwards to play. They daren't go near those swings because they are for the little 'uns and they are locked at half past seven. So there's nothing at all for him. He can't have no animals or plants. In a house they can have fun. When I was in Davidson Street I never saw my lad. He was out playing. The neighbours were good. In those side streets you always had crofts. You didn't have to go far for them. They played games. But when they get in these flats it's like prisons. These flats are all right for couples, older couples, those without kids.

Flats have the convenience of having everything on one floor. But I wouldn't advise anybody to come in a flat. If I was to do chips now I could still smell those chips even when I got into bed, on my bedclothes. In these flats you have to keep your bedroom windows open, otherwise they smell. But if you open the windows it lets the heat out.

DORIS MASON: *Nice but damp*

Mrs Doris Mason has one of the most attractive new council houses in the city. It was built by a nationally famous building firm. There are

roses growing in the front garden and sweet peas in the back garden.
The two downstairs rooms open into one. The style is modern, unlike
many Corporation houses. The houses of the four-year-old estate are
built round small closes to prevent traffic dangers.

We used to live in a terrible house, full of mice and all kinds of
vermin. I was very glad to move away from there. We moved into
the new flats, which took a bit of getting used to. For instance, not
being able to stand at your own front door as you did in your old
home. Eventually I got used to it and I really loved it. It was
lovely. I liked the electric underfloor heating, very cosy in the
winter. When I came home from work I could clean right through
that flat in an hour. After that the day was my own, to do my
shopping and cooking and go wherever I wanted to go.

It suited me but it didn't suit my husband. He wanted to move.
When we heard of these new houses being built near where we
had come from I applied on health grounds, and got one. The
house is very nice, it's smashing. The district is not so good.

It's a terraced house, with three bedrooms and a small back
garden. There's a bathroom, with a separate toilet, living-room,
dining-room and kitchen. Also a cubby hole and a small hall at the
entrance. There's this modern ranch fencing round the front, high
fencing too. I don't know whatever they put it there for. You've got
good cupboard space in the kitchen. It's a good shaped kitchen,
big enough to eat your meals in.

We were all right for the first twelve months. Then the dampness started creeping in, even though I do use my gas heating
throughout all the cold weather. That's thirty shillings a week,
every week of the year. And still it doesn't keep the dampness
away. I know there's a lot of people on the estate far worse off
than I am with the dampness. Although I do know a lot of them
don't use the heating as it should be used, because they have
to keep down the expense.

So I reported the damp and these two fellows came. They
scraped the walls first and then put this stuff on. They said
definitely that the green mould wouldn't come back. I waited for
twelve months before I put paper on the walls, to make sure. But
it has come back. The mould has come through the paper, as you have
seen. I've said that with it coming through the paper this time I
won't put paper on the walls again. You haven't got the heart to

do it. I'll just colour wash them in future. It's just upstairs. We don't have the trouble at all downstairs. My daughter, her husband and their baby sleep in that bedroom. They are waiting to go onto another estate.

I think the rents are too high, they are £4.80 a week. Then you've got this 30 shillings a week gas heating on top of that. For electric lighting and cooking with electricity I buy a pound's worth of stamps every week. That's £7.30 a week.

My husband is a milkman. I do office cleaning from six to eleven, five mornings a week, and go back on a Friday night to do three hours. We've just got a ten shillings rise, and that brings my wage to £8. So that just covers the cost of the house, heating and cooking.

I have heard they are bringing out some kind of a Bill in Parliament so that everyone who has money coming in should help those on a lower rate of pay. But those who are pushing this Bill through don't really understand. You've got crafty people on these estates. They are forging these income forms to the Council to get a rent rebate. They are getting jobs on the side, without stamping their cards. They can boast to you they have so much coming in the house, yet they are paying a low rent. How they do it I don't know. Of course your blood boils when you are paying a full rent, when you know they have more money coming in than you have. I think this Bill comes out in October. Any rate, my back is up against it. If it does go through I've said I'll change to a small terrace house that's not Corporation property before I'll pay the extra.

Otherwise I think these houses are beautiful. Some people do something with the garden. Others do nothing. I think flats are ideal living for a couple. They're not much good where there are children. Small children can't go out to play, their parents are too frightened to let them. I think flats should be kept for people with children in their teens, who are capable of looking after themselves, or for people with no family at all.

The flats were ideal for me, especially with electric central heating. But a lot of people spoil them because they don't keep them clean. They leave rubbish lying about. A few even urinate in the lifts. This is what it all boils down to – the way people use this living accommodation. It's not that they are scruffy when they are built: it's people that make them scruffy. It's the people that make them into slums. If people would take a bit more care of the

premises they are living in and make the children behave themselves a bit better, then I think everything would be fine with these
flats.

The Corporation put the houses up – the Labour Corporation,
because it was Labour controlled when this clearance started in
Salford. I don't think it would ever have started if they hadn't
been in. We've got them to thank for it.

But it's the people what make the slums. You've just seen it on
the estate as you walked up. The kids are all throwing sods of soil
about. The parents are inside. If they've seen them they just couldn't
care less. They just let them do as they like.

THOMAS JONES: *An architect's opinion*

*Thomas Jones, forty-three, is a successful architect, with experience of
contracts ranging from churches to council houses. He lives in a modern,
self-designed house, which he recently had built for himself and his
family, four miles from his office in the city centre.*

Damp in new properties is far more prevalent than most people
realise. It is a phenomenon of minor importance compared, say,
with a disaster such as that at the Ronan Point building collapse,
so that people come to live with it. Yet the personal inconvenience
involved can be very severe, at the worst from the health point of
view, apart from the sheer unpleasantness.

The occurrence of damp through condensation in the home is
often aesthetically objectionable by virtue of fungi and black
stains on walls. It is also practically difficult to live with when bed-
clothing and bed linen become damp, and when leatherware and
articles of clothing in cupboards become green-mouldy and
ruined. These, of course, are small in comparison with a Ronan
Point collapse. The latter situation demands a consideration of
the structural problems which led to that disaster, to the change of
legislation and codes of practice. But, if the cost of damp in homes
could be estimated, it would reduce the Ronan Point situation to
insignificance – and Ronan Point cost the country over fifty million

pounds. It would cost far more than that if a programme of remedying damp in all houses were undertaken.

The prevalence of damp goes back to 1945 and the beginning of post-war building. But there have not yet been very substantial efforts to come to grips with the problem. Only recently have we had the publication of the Ministry of Building and Public Works second bulletin on the matter. (Although a city architect told me recently that in his authority they had known of the problem and had been attempting to deal with it for over ten years.)

Why is damp arising in so many homes today? It exists in many older homes, for instance on the window sills. But in new homes people are much less inclined to tolerate it. Correctly so. One expects new properties to rid themselves of defects found in the older ones. Very often, too, in new homes, the dampness manifests itself in an ugly fashion, with dark, black or green fungus mould growths, which make the situation look much worse than it is from a technical point of view. So it is not a new phenomenon. What has changed is the frequency and the severity of the problem.

Why is damp arising in so many homes today? There are a number of interrelated reasons. Firstly, because we live in more affluent times there is a much higher standard of comfort by means of central heating. Condensation results from moisture suspended in the air depositing itself on cold surfaces. The warmer the temperature of the air the greater the amount of moisture the air holds in suspension, and the greater the deposit if it meets a cold surface, such as the walls and windows. The moisture arises through people's breath and kitchen and bathroom activities.

Another fact is that ventilation in present days is not so readily achieved as it used to be in older properties. They used to have chimneys, and whether there was a fire or not, they acted as a constant ventilator. In modern buildings we don't normally have fireplaces. In any case, the British concern to avoid draughts is one of our national traditions. Anything that gets rid of draughts is welcomed, though one man's draughts is another person's ventilation. The design of some windows in modern flats makes it impossible to open them by such a small amount as to make it acceptable. Large panes of glass, together with an insensitivity to control of the opening, so that the smallest opening you can have lets in the rain or a howling gale, means that most people are inclined to leave the windows shut.

A further reason is the changing social pattern in which, more often than was ever the case, the woman of the house seeks to supplement the total income by going out to work during the day. So the house is not occupied during the day, as it used to be. It is left to cool. Then both husband and wife come home and the first thing they do is to raise the heat temperature as quickly as possible, which instantly creates the worst conditions for the deposition of condensation. The house, the walls, and the plaster and painted surfaces are cold. Instantly the heat is turned on. Cooking takes place. And the degree of condensation deposit is rapid and dramatic. So here is another cause of dampness which is probably unique to the present time.

There are a number of more subtle reasons why condensation is rampant today. For example, the preponderance of new techniques in building design. Due to the pressure to build at minimum costs, structures have been erected without full knowledge of the physical limitations of certain systems, as far as condensation and thermal insulation are concerned. Very often the form and character of these systems are fathered by engineers to whom the height and the stability of the building are paramount considerations. But chances are taken – often for the best reasons – to try and advance the cause of housing. But clearly the homework was never done fully, if the implications of new methods were not thought all the way through, so far as the cross section of the wall construction was concerned. Usually prefabrication systems are, by the nature of their construction, relatively thin compared with traditional brickwork. So heat losses take place more rapidly. And the higher they go, the more exposed the sites, the worse are the problems.

When houses are built together traditionally they shelter one another from high winds. Therefore the degree of exposure is minimal in normal urban settings. But you find that multi-storey blocks are usually set at much greater distances from one another, as well as being higher in the air. I'm thinking particularly of overspill estates. Some of the new towns are badly exposed to the winds. So the outside conditions are very much worse.

Then there is what is called the cold bridge – a horizontal beam inside the building bringing cold from outside to the inside of the structure.

The remedial problem is a very vexatious one. If only because the problem shows itself in so many different forms. The identification of the exact cause in different dwellings is tedious and almost impracticable over the whole range of the problem. It may take a Council several years from the first report of the problem to the time they can decide what to do about it.

There are certain simple rules about the way in which the property is used: ensuring that ventilation is available and is used and that the prime causes of moisture in the air are cut down; seeing that kitchen doors are closed when cooking takes place and windows in the kitchen are left open, and that bathroom steam is not allowed to percolate into the house. More important is to raise the temperature of the house and keep it, more or less, at that temperature throughout the day. Consistent temperatures keep the brickwork and plaster surfaces to a higher temperature constantly.

We are all aware of the high cost of putting central heating into buildings which don't have it or of running heating systems throughout the day for people who are out at work. A higher degree of thermal insulation in the external walls becomes a necessary parallel measure, so that the walls do not lose the additional heat to the outside air. Sometimes it is easier and less costly to add to the thermal value of the wall rather than to have a heating system which is good but takes no measures to prevent the loss of that valuable heat. It is possible to insulate the walls after the building had been completed, but very often only at inconvenience and at quite some cost. I.C.I. have a plastic material which is used to line the internal face of walls. But the fact still remains that the application of this is a messy and costly business.

How to prevent this happening in future buildings? The most imperative step is to educate the architect, the builder and the building technicians so that they know fully the technical aspects of the problem. So they can come to terms more completely with the problem at the drawing-board stage. It is difficult to reach a large body of people voluntarily through the normal media. I think there is a gradual realisation in the professions that this is something which must be given closer consideration.

Should there be closer governmental inspection? Architects already have to show many more drawings for scrutiny than we sometimes think are necessary. But I do feel that, whilst building inspectors and their departments do spend a great deal of time in scrutinising plans submitted for approval under the building regulations, it seems incredible that the new building regulations introduced in 1965 or any subsequent amendments have not introduced some feature enabling the local authority to check that the construction of the wall and roof are adequate from the condensation aspect. It is possible by submitting a specification of the construction of the wall and ceiling, and by describing the use of the building, as to whether it is residential or bathroom or kitchen, for town hall officials by using empirical methods to check whether the structure will comply.

So, though I am always reluctant to add yet another check on the professional man's work, I do believe it needs a move of that kind. The representatives of the City or Borough Architects are the buildings inspectors who check drawings, even now, as regards structural stability, the provision of damp proof courses, the heights of ceilings and the safeness of stairways. Perhaps it would be deemed to be practicable to introduce another measure ensuring that someone had the statutory duty to check that the building in its cross sectional character would be satisfactory from the point of view of condensation.

GRAHAM STODDARD: *Children in trouble*

Graham Stoddard has a tiny office in a big new secondary school for boys. From one window he can see the long rows of old two-up, two-down, slum houses. On the other side the twenty-storey blocks of council flats soar to the skies. They are his territory. From the office he pays his visits to the homes of the children attending (or often failing to attend) the school. Graham is a child care welfare officer.

Leaving school at 15, he joined the police force, although anyone looking less like a policeman would be difficult to find. He is thin, pale, neatly dressed. It was his police experience with juvenile delinquents which originally brought him into social work. He became fed up with locking people up and took a university course in social work by correspondence. He is now thirty-five.

If you ask the children living in the flats – and we do ask them – what they would most like to see, they say, 'Open spaces with some trees; a place where we can play football; and somewhere we can keep pets.'

The children have a deep need to keep pets. Pigeon stealing is a common offence. They find them in the outer areas of the city. They are continually bringing stray cats and dogs to school.

Pets are not allowed in the flats. There was one flat where the family never let me enter. I found out later the reason: they had got a cat and they thought that I might give their secret away. It is important that children should be able to care for pets. So this school is starting a pigeon loft. But surely the planners should provide such things in the area. They never think of consulting the children – and seldom their parents either. These buildings are now completed. It's too late for them. In future, however, they must consider this kind of thing.

I was born in a country village and played by the river and on the farms and in the fields. These kids can't play anywhere – except in front of a motor-car. I take some of them to a farm in the hills twenty miles away. The other day one little boy asked me if he could feed the pigs, 'the woolly ones down there'. He meant lambs, which he had never seen before.

Recently I had a fourteen year old boy whose parents had to pay a fine of three pounds ten shillings. He had blocked the lift with a pregnant woman stuck in it. She was in a terrible state. When I went into the matter, it was evident that the boy was misbehaving through boredom. He said to me, 'We live in a land of "don'ts" round here.'

Yet there is a magnificent gymnasium in this school, only a few yards away. It is not for use in the evening – as it should be. Similarly there is nowhere for the boys to play football when there's a fine big schoolyard here which is empty after school hours. When the children started playing in it policemen were actually sent to turn them out. I believe adventure playgrounds would be valuable too. You would need supervision in both these cases. Instead of talking about community schools we should make them so. If we did we wouldn't have so much vandalism.

One of the best things about these new estates is that they are smoke-free zones. The clean air has proved a big advantage, healthwise in particular. The amount of chestiness and colds and bronchitis is going down fast. Our school records prove it. One lad said to me, 'Did you know that sparrows are brown, sir?' Previously he had only seen blackened ones.

There are other good features of the new flats. The standard of cleanliness and upkeep of the home goes up when the family moves in. It may relapse in some cases after about a year. 'It's smashing', they say, without realising all the problems. For they like to get new furniture, and in any case the housing authority won't let them take rotten old furniture into these apartments. But they are subjected to TV advertising and no deposit, so they buy flashy furniture which often drops to pieces after three months or so. They can't replace it because they are up to their eyes in hire purchase payments on the recently purchased furnishings.

The debts begin to mount up. The rents are higher. Huge gas and electric bills arrive. We had a case of a father of one of our children faced with a fuel bill for £142! He was on a low wage. We tried various charities without success. In the end the father solved the problem himself – by a big win on the horses!

Some residents get so frightened about which debt collector will next be knocking on the door or ringing the bell that they refuse to answer callers at all. And it's much harder in these flats to tell from outside the door whether there is anybody in or not. Sometimes this seclusion builds up and the tenants never go out at all.

What can you do about these gas, electricity and other bills? The heating undertakings say, 'We're not running a charity.' And I suppose that's correct. Perhaps better wages for the low paid is the only answer.

Some people like to live in flats even though they don't want to go in them at first. But there is a minority who really do suffer. When they move to the tower blocks many develop headaches, lack of interest in sex, and general aches and pains. This applies whether they are on the ground floor or at the top. And this happens too often to newcomers to be a coincidence. Sometimes these ills go; sometimes they persist.

The new areas are going to create new problems. For example, the feeling of isolation; or the uniformity of the dwellings. There's a story going round here about a man who came home a bit drunk. He went to the wrong flat and, of course, found his key didn't fit. So he put his shoulder to the door and shoved. He walked in and got into bed – without noticing he was in someone else's house.

Then there are things like the lifts always breaking down. These may be small things but they accumulate into big ones. They lead to frustration.

There are schools in this area where one in four of the children who leave at fifteen cannot read or write. This is a tremendous problem in most industrial cities. In a single month I had twenty-two separate school leavers who approached me self-consciously and asked if they could see me in private. I found that, one by one, each had the same request to make: 'Will you fill in this form for me?'

These are not mentally backward children. They have average intelligence quotients. If a boy can't read he gets bored at school. He talks to his mate and gets kicked out of the class. This is partly the fault of the schools. But there is little provision of room in their homes which would help them to do their homework. The rooms are still small, even if they are bigger than in the old terraced properties.

Another thing we encounter – as in other industrial towns – is a massive truancy problem. We have started a scheme of using youth centres for therapeutic groups to solve some of these problems. In a recent month no less than £2,700 loss was caused by theft or damage by thirty-one children. It was wrong to assume they were from slum homes. They came from the new flats too, and not from the top flats, because there are few small children there. Nor was there any correlation with the fathers' jobs. It was more often connected with creeping mental illness in the mother.

We had a serious truancy situation in a block of very old and unsuitable dwellings, where some very large families had been housed. Instead of hounding the parents about their children's bad attendance we just met them to discuss their problems. Some of the families had nine or ten children. A number of the mothers had three or four toddlers with them all the time and hardly ever went out. Occasionally they went out with their husband, leaving the little ones with an older child, but feeling guilty about doing so. This guilt feeling sometimes led them to spoiling the children and buying them endless ice-creams.

We found a natural born leader amongst the mothers and got her to run an informal sort of playgroup in a church hall nearby. This allowed an hour's shopping time. School attendance went up right away. We had all these children attending school together for the first time. The playgroup is still going. Playgroups are vital. Accommodation must be provided for them on all new estates. But the designers and architects still talk about 'housing units' – not homes. No one thinks about putting a teacher or a parent on the planning boards.

I'd like to say something about the housing in quite different sorts of places: seaside resorts like Scarborough and Whitby, near where I was born. Most people think of these as 'nice places', For many of the residents they are, but not for all. There are ghettoes in these towns which are a disgrace, which are the acme of social injustice.

In Scarborough the worse the difficulties a family got into, the higher up the hill they went. Conditions were so bad near the top, with broken glass lying about, that social workers wouldn't take their cars there. Some of the powers that be were only concerned with where they could get rid of these poor families. They were so mercenary that people didn't count. I remember ordering something on hire purchase, which I don't usually do. It was a special chair. The hire purchase firm would not accept the order. They told me, 'You are in a high risk area.' Those tenants who get into arrears with their rents are moved into the ghetto. If, after a few weeks there, they are still in arrears, they are put out.

As for the rural areas, some of the families live in conditions worse than city slums. I know houses today where they have to get all their water from a well. And they can't even do that when it's frozen. The countryman doesn't shout, or know who to shout to. If he's a farm labourer living in a tied cottage he doesn't dare to shout.

6. Life on the land: in a tied cottage

JOE BRAMLEY

*Joe is a cowman working on a farm in a village near Malton in the
North Riding of Yorkshire. He is lean and wiry, with dark curly hair
and plenty of colour in his cheeks. Today he has taken the afternoon
off, and is smartly dressed in a green sports jacket and trousers, and a
neat yellow shirt and tie.*

I've lived all my married life in tied cottages. That means a house
which is tied to the job. If you lose your job you lose your home too.

I got married when I was twenty-four in a village called
Stokesley in Cleveland. We lived with her mother and father
for about six months. They were in a tied house at that time.
Her father had been a farm worker for thirty-five years.

My wife and I decided to strike out on our own. So I got a job
in another village and went into a terraced house there, belonging to the farmer. It had an earth closet. When I went there I was
allowed a day to clean this place out with a horse and cart. There
was about two loads of somebody else's rubbish in, you see. Otherwise we couldn't use it.

These earth closets are usually surrounded by a brick wall,
three to four foot high. This contains ashes *etcetera* that keeps
everything dry. It means you only have to make a good clean out
once every six months or so. Against that you've got rats. You
were often adjoining a field, and you were never far from farm
buildings, which of course harbour rats and mice. It was very
crude, but in the flush of getting married and a home on our own
and looking forward to great things, it was all right. I got over it
by just using a bucket and burying it weekly in the garden, as we
had a big garden.

In that house we only had one child. I've got nine today. They're
good children and I've a lot to be thankful for. There's none of
them in farming. I didn't really encourage them to go in for farm

work. That doesn't mean that I never found farming interesting. I do. But it's hard work, for so little return. I found a satisfaction in the job. It was the economics of it that I discovered over many years as my family grew up.

We had a little dispute after we had been in that house for eighteen months which didn't result in my losing the job or the house immediately, but it made me see what being in a tied cottage could mean.

It was like this. I was working as a general farm labourer. The cowman wanted to go on his holidays for a few days. I was able to do this job and I was pressed into it. I said, 'All right, I'll do it'. I liked the lad and he was as entitled to his time off as anybody else. So away he went. Now the men each got a pint of free milk a day, or more according to their cans, some of which held a pint and a half. Whichever can they put out we used to fill it with milk. Generously I filled them all up. The young boss' wife decided I had been too generous with the milk, so she would halve everybody's milk and give them half of what they usually got. Though why she should choose this particular time to do it I wouldn't really know. So I got the backlash of all this. 'Never had this happened before,' they said, 'Old John never used to do this', and so on. I told her that they wouldn't grumble at me any more as this would be the last time I'd do that particular man's job. I said what I had to say and we got over that difficulty. My wife and I never got any more milk, and that was one of the supposed perks of my house.

We didn't pay any cash rent for the house. We did week-end work instead. When we lost that pint of milk we lost the so-called perks.

Everything quietened down, though things were never quite the same. Then, a couple of years later, came the bigger dispute. The same cowman wanted his holidays again. They said, 'You go and milk.' I said, 'No.' I reminded them I said I would never do that job again. Then we had a bit of a to-do. They said, 'If you won't go and milk you'll have to take a fortnight's notice. And we want the house.'

We had two sons by then, a baby and one nearly three. That was in November. It's a bad time of the year to get jobs. In that village the farmer had put the pressure on to prevent anyone giving me a job. The farmers would give me a casual job for a day or so, but some of them admitted to me that they daren't even do that, because the farmer had told them not to. They felt they couldn't afford to fall out with somebody whom they could borrow something off in the near future, say an implement. There was nothing official.

From time to time he'd come down the hill and say, 'Bramley, you'll have to get out of this house, you know.' I was out of work from November to February. I was still in the house but the pressure was constantly on. You felt there was hostility towards you in the village. Another reason he wanted me out of the house was that he had to pay rates on it, till it was empty.

I didn't want to trouble my parents for help, because they were ill. As for the in-laws I didn't feel I'd get much sympathy from them because I had stood up for principles. My father-in-law was always very kind and sympathised with me. But he was in the same position. He'd eaten enough humble pie in thirty odd years to choke himself.

I did go and find jobs for odd days outside the village. We lived on a knife edge, but we existed. Then in February I got another job in a village near Skipton. This was for a doctor. As far as farming went he hadn't a clue. I went there as a stockman. I could see that the cattle were getting enough feeding, but not the correct feeding. By changing it I got some results which amazed the doctor. Then he sold the farm and that brought me down to earth again. A young farmer took over.

I was living in a tied cottage that was absolutely devoid of facilities. It was a smaller house than before. But it offered an escape from the job where I had had the trouble. We felt we were in a happier situation and that we might alter the house in the future.

However, I ought mention that we only had the one earth toilet between the two adjoining houses. The toilet had a double seat. I don't know if we were expected to sit side by side on it! In this case there was a rural district service which would empty it for us. I didn't envy them the task in this instance; it was a terror of a place. We never did, by the way, go and sit alongside our neighbours on it!

I was very interested in the job, and so that compensated me, but it didn't compensate my wife. Though we did eventually manage to get an electric boiler in, even if it cost us the earth.

Before we got that we had a nasty accident. Through lack of facilities, we boiled water on the fire. One evening four of the children were all getting bathed in front of the fire, getting ready for bed. Robert got pushed back onto this pan, hitting the handle of it, and the boiling water went right down his back. This was the first serious accident we had ever had. We were fortunate with the doctor. There wasn't one in the village, but I phoned up and a doctor came from four miles away in a few minutes. Robert was in the hospital within the hour. We had reduced a lot of the damage with powder, but we had missed one place, near his privates. Because of our ignorance he was in hospital for two months longer than he need have been.

When he got better we were reasonably content. The work, as I say, was interesting. The wage was three pounds a week up on what we had had previously, which had been about five pounds a week. I eventually ended up with about nine pounds a week there. We paid no actual rent and had no rent book. Nevertheless it was counted, in a roundabout sort of way, as a perk, as you might say. You had milk and a garden and a certain amount of freedom.

I was engrossed in the job and not fully aware of the implications of the housing problem. It only hit me from time to time, when you came home at night and found how indelicate things were.

Maybe for a long time you forget about the house because you get so interested in the job. It's the wife, who spends most of her life in the home, that worries about the house. All goes smoothly until there comes a dispute between the farmer and the man. And then, suddenly, the worker realises how dependent he is, that he will lose not just his job but his house too.

Eventually the farmer found he couldn't farm the whole place as it was. So he went into turkeys, and sold the rest off. The new farmer was a bit of a pusher and was bringing his own brothers to help him out. I felt that this wasn't the position I was wanting, and I'd enjoyed five years of almost being my own boss. So I moved on.

The next house was a tied house too. I had only worked at this farm for ten months when I went down with the worst dose of 'flu I'd ever had. I thought I had got better but when I got out of bed I dropped like a stone. So I crawled back into bed. The result was I had to have a fortnight off. I should have had three weeks. I went back to work, which was a stupid thing to do. I went on a

stack the following day and, unfortunately, pulling out some
straw, the band snapped and I fell backwards, over the top of a
bundle onto the stone yard. This put me off work again with
terribly bruised ribs. This was a month off at a stretch. So the
farmer came down to me and said, 'I'm sorry, I can't do with a
man that is going to be off. You'll have to take your notice. I'll
give you a month just to find a place.'

I felt really down. I was beginning to realise that the situation
was never really going to improve. However, I got another job later,
again living in a tied house, but with all modern cons. It was a
big place with rather a high rent. But now we come to what was
really an official union dispute. I've been a member of the Agricultural Workers' Union since I was twenty. I'm a branch chairman
today.

The union had got an hour knocked off for farm workers on a
Saturday morning, so that we should finish at eleven o'clock instead
of at mid-day. So the next week-end this farmer came along to
me at twenty past eleven and said, 'What are you doing?' I was
putting my clothes on. I said, 'We should have been finished at
eleven o'clock this morning. You know what the union says: the
shorter working week.' He said, 'But *I* didn't say so. I don't accept
it. If you don't carry on till twelve o'clock, you're finished.' I asked
him if he realised he was causing a union dispute. He didn't care.
So that was the end of that job.

The union fought the case for me. They took it to the County
Court. We were given a short stay by the Court so we could look
for another house. I am happy to say that in this place the local
authority was sympathetic. They fixed us up with a council house.
Some local authorities go out of their way to provide houses for
farm workers living in tied cottages. But others don't. They won't
even accept on to their waiting lists those living in tied houses. For
you usually find that, in country districts, the councils are dominated
by farmers, land-owners and their friends.

The union is having to spend a lot of money fighting evictions
in the courts. I believe they took legal action in sixty cases last
month alone.

Take the case of another farm worker I knew. He got a job
on a farm and secured this tied house for his father and mother
to live in, along with himself. They had retired and had nowhere
to live, as they had previously lived in tied houses. He couldn't

get them a cottage to rent. The farmer and my friend agreed, never thinking there would be a dispute in the future. Then the dispute arose, union-wise, over Bank Holidays. This Bank Holiday clashed with the harvest. The man said he was entitled to have the holiday on that particular day, because he wanted to go somewhere special. Then the farmer said, 'Well, you'll have to give up that house that your mother and father is in.' Being a young man he could get another job, but his mother and father was left there. The farmer cut off one entrance and just left them a dirty entrance, ploughed up with cattle.

Then there was another case near here where the worker, a union member, got sacked, but the Court gave them a respite to stay in the house. It was a house with oil-fired central heating. The oil ran out during this period, which was mid-winter. So, although there were kiddies, the farmer wouldn't replenish the oil, in order to drive them out of the house.

The union is against the tied cottage for two reasons: It holds down wages, and it causes fear and anxiety. The fear of having your roof taken away is even worse than that of losing your job. Often the wife becomes more frightened than the husband. Sometimes the farmer may come and see her when the farm hand is at work. He may threaten her with cutting off the electricity.

The farmers may argue that where a farm is isolated they need to have a worker living on it to look after the cattle or deal with calving. Things are different today, for with motor-cycles or scooters or motor-cars they don't have to live on the job.

. . . in London

7. Bad housing, bad health, bad wages

MARY LEMON · JEAN YOUNG · DORIS KENNET ·
ROSE JACKSON

MARY LEMON: *The rich and the poor*

*Mrs Mary Lemon and her husband and son live in the basement of a
large terraced house typical of thousands in Paddington, Kensington,
Chelsea, Islington, and other parts of London. The whole house was
once (before the last war) occupied by a single family and their servants.
There are four floors and a basement, all of them crammed with inhabitants. Next door, where the decorators are in and the ground floor
temporarily vacant, the owners have had to put a notice in the window
saying, 'No flats to let', so intense is the pressure for accommodation.*

*The broad avenue stretches for nearly half a mile. At one end live
the poor people, like Mrs Lemon; at the other live very well-to-do
families. The juxtaposition is sharp, with the appearance of trees at one
end indicating the changed income of the residents. Nearby, luxurious
mansions overlook 'Little Venice', as the Paddington Canal is known.*

*Mary, who is nearing sixty, is very stout. On the table lies a thick
walking stick, which she takes with her everywhere. She is as pale as
the basement is dark.*

I've had this arthritis for ten years, and periodically I have treatment for it, although it doesn't seem to have much effect. The cause
of it is the damp house we live in. We've had the Sanitary Inspector
and many people from the Council looking it over. They promised
to make it a proper modernised basement and put the damp right,
but we have had no success. We have a little room with a bath in
it. It's very awkward, because with me being so disabled I have
great difficulty in getting in and out of the bath.

The ceiling is so dilapidated it keeps on falling in. The cement
comes in big chunks, which make it very dangerous. They might
hit me on the head. I'm always afraid. Somebody has to be in the
house when I do have a bath.

The steps are very awkward because they have such a turn at the top. Two people have to help me, with a hand under each arm. They promised to put a rail on either side so that I could help myself up by these rails. Then I could try and go for a little walk outside, you see.

My husband's health is pretty bad, too. He suffers from bronchial asthma and also from ulcers. This makes him in and out of work. He's under the chest hospital at Brompton. When his ulcers get very bad he is rushed to St Mary's Hospital. He was in there for treatment about six weeks ago. He gets about £20 a week, leaving about £15 to bring home after all his stoppages. I'm totally dependent on him because I don't get anything from any society or anybody at all. I have to eke out the money the best way I can. It makes us pretty tight – we don't have many luxuries with it.

We have two rooms, one kitchen and a bathroom. You couldn't call it a proper bathroom – it's just a little room with a bath in it. Our rent is £2 19s 4d a week, because we have been here twenty-six years this January and so are controlled tenants. It's an unfurnished flat. We can't be turned out – again because we are controlled tenants. The lady above us is in another controlled flat. She's also on a low rent. Above her the remaining half of the house is let off to a whole crowd of hippies. The rooms are let off individually at an extortionate rent. They pay about eighteen guineas for that floor. Above them is a darkie and his wife and they pay a terrible rent.

They are all furnished up there. Appallingly furnished, you know.

The landlord hasn't actually told us he wants to get us out, but you can see he does. He keeps promising and promising to do the place up. He keeps sending the builder here and gives us the hint that we'd have to get out whilst the job was done. If we did get out that would break our contract and he'd never let us in again, unless we paid, say, twenty guineas a week, because we've got a good garden. Many people would pay a lot for the good garden. He wants to get moneyed people in here. They would not be controlled tenants like us. There's no control for future tenants. He'd easy get twenty guineas a week for this because it's in a good neighbourhood here in Maida Vale. Film stars live in the mansions around here.

Two old maiden ladies used to live next door in one of these flats. They had been there ever since they were born. A new land-lord came in. He got a room in Forest Hill for the two old ladies, whilst the house next door was being done. It was very badly dilapidated. The roof had fallen in and the first floor was all in, and there was a great bath under the next floor, which the tenants had put there to catch the water when it rained. The poor old things had no money to repair it. They were away for six months. It cost the landlord thousands to get it converted. He let them come back and they were on the first floor at a much higher rent. In the basement he charges about fifteen guineas – and that was a couple of years ago. It will be more now. The idea is to get us out and to get other tenants in at fifteen or twenty guineas a week, which they would get easy, because it's such a select neighbourhood.

It's eight years since we first applied for a council flat. Before that I was working nights at Willesden Hospital for seven years and the two children were small. So I couldn't pursue the matter as I would like to have done, to be at them to be out of this and into a new flat. They have done nothing about it. I got so tired of filling in this card they send you each year that I left off doing so. Then they didn't bother at all. I didn't hear anything at all until Mr Latham the MP came on the scene, who took my case up. He's done marvellous for me.

The Sanitary Inspector used to come here and look around carefully. Not a chimney would work. The flat was full of damp. It seemed to be coming up from the foundations. Everything was very musty. The clothes were damp in the bedroom. But the council officials said there were thousands worse off than we were.

We have a big mice run under the kitchen floor, from the door to the hole where they come out. We had the man here from the Council putting poison down.

If I could have my choice I'd like a nice little bungalow, a ground floor one. I don't think I'd like these high flats. I'd like a little garden with the bungalow.

(*Mrs Lemon laughs. The idea of someone like herself getting a bungalow seems plain ridiculous.*)

4*

JEAN YOUNG: *How can we buy?*

Mrs Young, pretty, dark-haired, pale-faced, is in her mid-twenties.
When I first met her she was standing at the gate, knitting. What she
was really more concerned about was keeping an eye on her two little
boys, Chris and Alex, to see they didn't run onto the road. The two
boys were playing happily on the pavement with a group of English,
Cypriot and West Indian children from neighbouring multi-storey
houses.

I have been living in the present accommodation for about six
years. I know that the houses round her are due for redevelopment,
owing to the fact that they are in a bad condition. In the house
that we live in two families share one bath and one toilet, and we
share the toilet with the people upstairs, which, of course, is inconvenient when you have children. My husband works for the newspapers, selling them to the retail newsagents. There are five families
altogether in the house. There is a garden, but it's only available
for the people in the basement, so the children can't use it.

The children play in the street, which of course I mind. Because
of the traffic it's dangerous. There is an adventure playground not
far way, but there was an accident two weeks ago, with a child
seriously injured, so I don't allow them to play there. The recreation
ground isn't too far away. I sometimes take them there in the
afternoon. One of the children goes to a holiday club now during
the school holidays. One is five and one is four. There is friction
caused amongst neighbours when you have children, because the
flats aren't self-contained. Having to share other amenities causes
this.

We have tried several agents to try and buy a house. At the present
moment there aren't any houses being built round here. Consequently there are fewer for sale, and those that are being sold
are going for exorbitant prices. We tried nearly eighteen months
ago to buy a house off the North Circular Road, a family house
with five rooms. But at that time they wanted £5,000. Now, of
course, a house in that road in that area would cost about £7,000
to £7,500. Therefore you would need two thousand to two and a
half thousand deposit, at least, to put down.

We are still trying to see if we can possibly buy a house in

Cricklewood or Neasden or that locality. Because even if we applied for a council house there are so many on the list that we would come at the very end, and it would be years before we would get anything. So we think the best thing for us is to try and buy our own.

If we did buy a house it would be a two-family house, having a bathroom and toilet on each floor. Therefore you could let the top and live on the ground.

In the flat we are living in now there are two rooms and a kitchen, which has a bath in it. We share the toilet upstairs. I know that in the redevelopment there will have to be a separate bathroom, since they don't allow baths in the kitchen any more. We do use the bath, but in the new stipulations you have to have the bath separate from the kitchen, and you have to have hot water as well – which we haven't got. We have to heat hot water on the gas stove, though we have a geyser over the bath.

We only have one bedroom, which the children share with us. We would like two bedrooms, which would be more convenient, as they are growing up now, and they do need their own room.

They have rats next door. We have mice – we caught them in traps. We can't have a cat because they keep birds upstairs.

Yesterday we went along to the housing authority about the house we live in, which is due for auction. Apparently in the redevelopment, if each flat costs £500 to re-do, the Council pays half. If it's £200 the Council pays half, according to what has to be done. This includes a toilet, bathroom, kitchen and hot and cold water in each flat. Also the electric wiring has to be up to the standard of today. This could mean that a five-floor house would come to about two and a half thousand pounds having to be spent on it. The rents, of course, would go up, but in yearly stages of 7s 6d a time, as far as I know – 37½p. At present we pay £3. If things were put into the flat to make the conditions better it would be worth paying a little bit more, even if after three years it had gone up by 22s 6d a week.

We wouldn't mind being rehoused, but the multi-storey council flats near us are so exorbitantly high. They look too dangerous to me to have children. It would frighten me. Even to leave them playing in the street and look down on them from such a height would be nerve-breaking. I do know of several people who have had nervous breakdowns through this. They live maybe on the seventeenth floor and their children are on the ground floor, playing. The mothers have to go to the doctor's for tablets for their nerves. It's just frustrating. Therefore I wouldn't like the same thing to happen to me.

Even if we did have a council flat we'd have to pay about nine guineas a week, which is the case in this area. I would rather have my own house. If I had to pay nine guineas that, at least, would pay the mortgage. And in the majority of cases round here of a man earning £20 to £25 a week, if he was paying nine guineas a week, how could he possibly save money to buy a house? The cost of houses is going up year by year. Therefore he'd have to put more deposit down. So he never could save.

The two houses on this side have been sold and are now a hotel for tourists. As far as I know this house and the one next door, which has four large families in it, are also going to be sold to the same owner for the same purpose. Why? Because there is more money in it.

DORIS KENNET: *Landlords and children*

Doris Kennet, whose husband has left her, lives with her baby in a single basement room. Immediately outside her door stand seven dustbins from the other families in the terraced house. They smell in hot weather. With her large spectacles she has something of the look of a young school teacher. On the table is a typewriter.

I have one medium-sized room, of which one corner is partitioned off as my kitchen. I pay £6 a week, plus gas and electricity, which comes to about another pound. I share a bathroom and toilet with one other family. They have a room the same as mine and one bedroom. They pay £9.50. So that means that there's £15.50 rent coming just from the tenants in this basement. And there is also £15.50 being paid by two tenants for similar accommodation on the ground floor. I don't know how much they pay on the higher floors.

Sharing a bathroom and toilet can be very inconvenient for various sorts of reasons. In my particular case the young boy next door doesn't flush the toilet. This is rather an inconvenience. If the neighbours have parties you can walk into the toilet – and find someone is there.

This is a furnished flat. The furniture is very old and could have been picked up for about £20 at the most. Anything that looks old is theirs. I have added various things, like my own fridge, sofa, coffee table and television set. Really you get the barest essentials in a furnished flat. They don't provide things like crockery or cutlery or sheets. I have a landlord, but the Church Commissioners own the land. The Church Commissioners own all the houses round here and they lease them to various landlords, and they in turn put people in for these exorbitant rents.

There's a telephone in the front hall, on which some people have phone calls at 5.30 in the morning. They have an alarm call from the GPO because the husband has to go out at that time in the morning. This rings every morning. I can hear it and the whole house can hear it. It wakes me and the baby and the whole house. There have been complaints about this to the landlord, but nothing has been done about it so far.

I've put my name down on the Westminster housing list, but I have no priority. I'm on the deferred list, and this means I can wait anything up to ten or twenty years to get a house.

I've also tried private landlords. But they really don't want children, and I've a daughter of eighteen months. I'd really like somewhere with a garden, because where we are now she has absolutely no place to play, as we don't have access to the garden at the back of the house. The only place she'll be able to play when she is older is on the streets, which is not very convenient for anyone.

Landlords don't want children because they seem to think that children create noise for their other tenants, maybe old tenants who don't like the noise that children make. Possibly they think that children might damage the walls or something like this. To me these reasons are all very petty. I don't know where children live in London. From my own experience it's very difficult. The only thing that happens if they take children is that they seem to up the rent. You know you are in for a flat at, say, £7 a week. As soon as you mention the child they say, 'That one isn't suitable for a child, but we do have one at eleven guineas.' Therefore, for most families this price is way out of their range.

ROSE JACKSON: *Mice, but no sanitation*

Mrs Rose Jackson comes from St Vincent, in the West Indies. Her problems are almost identical with those of white tenants in the neighbourhood. She is married with a husband and two children sharing one living-room and two bedrooms. Two of the flats in the house are occupied. The other two floors are vacant. She believes that the landlord wishes to get them out too, so he can sell the house with vacant possession.

Though the rooms are nicely kept, with wedding and family photos on the walls, there is no usable bath and no hot water. This house and the adjoining one are occupied by West Indian families. She takes the children to neighbours when they have a bath.

There used to be twenty-one of us living in this house, with one lavatory for all of us to use. I could hardly believe it at first. Most of the time I've got to go next door to use the toilet because we can't get inside ours. It's a problem to use it, especially when the children are home from school.

The kitchen is actually underneath the toilet. The sewage water from the toilet came down into the cooker where I cook. Most of the time I have to complain about it. It has been done now, but even now it's not properly done. You know they just kind of rough it up.

I pay £5 a week for this unfurnished flat. My husband has made a good job of it, but it's not very nice in the other rooms. I wouldn't like a Mulberry Trust house. The rents are too high. My husband earns about £22 a week bring home wage. He drives for the NCL, that's the National Carriers. Out of that I pay £5 a week rent. I couldn't afford anything more than that.

We had quite a lot of mice upstairs. In fact we had quite a lot of them through the whole house. It was terrible. They used to stand up looking at us, and when they see us they run.

If the Council fixed the house and gave us a bathroom I wouldn't mind staying here. I don't think they have enough space for a bathroom, the flat is so small. There is an existing bath in one of the rooms, but it is not connected. If they could fix that up I would like it. I'd be quite happy.

I won't like to remove out of the area. I like it here. I've got quite a lot of friends here. In fact I've been living in this area for ten years.

I spend well over £10 a week on food. I take £10 to make shopping. Then on Tuesdays I have to take another £2 to buy meat to keep me for the week. It's very expensive.

8. 'Rachman Road'

GLADYS EDMONDSON · PHILIP FENDER · JIM KELLY
BETTY HOOPER

This is one of the worst streets in the district. The four-storey tenements are over a hundred years old, all owned by two landlords, who are estimated to be making £7,500 a year, clear, out of the properties. The tenants, who have formed an active tenants' association, believe the buildings will come down about 1973.

These dwellings contain almost every housing defect: damp, vermin, overcrowding, lack of lavatories and bathrooms, rotting walls and ceilings, faulty drains. Yet many of the tenants have somehow managed to keep their homes clean and decent. They have spent much time, labour and money in redecorating, repairing, furnishing and everlastingly cleaning their rooms.

Surrounding the long row of rotting tenements and looking down on them are blocks of modern, fifteen-storey council flats. It is galling for the inhabitants of 'Rachman Road', who envy their neighbours in the tower blocks – at least in most respects.

GLADYS EDMONDSON: *One tap, four families*

She has the largest family and the worst overcrowding in the street. A part-time cleaner, she gets up at five o'clock to be at work for six. Yet of all the mothers here she is the livest wire. She sits at the table drinking a mid-morning cup of tea in a tiny living-cum-bedroom, which is hopelessly jammed with good furniture.

I've got five children, a ten-month-old baby, five-year-old twins, a fourteen-year-old boy and a sixteen-year-old girl.

The baby's got a cot in the corner and we've got a double bed in the centre. The twins have got bunk beds, which are very unsafe because one of the twins keeps falling out of the top bunk. You can't put the baby to sleep until the twins are in bed, because they keep waking her up. It means that the baby can't go to bed until about half past nine or ten o'clock in the summer. You can't get the twins earlier in the evening when the weather's nice. In the winter they go to bed earlier, but they don't go to sleep, because – being twins – they are skylarking about all the time.

As regards the two older ones, the girl, who's sixteen, sleeps at the top of a put-you-up settee in the living-room, whilst the boy, who's fourteen, sleeps at the bottom. We don't want her to get married yet – not at her age. But, the way things are going, she'll probably want to get out quick, because what young girl wants to stay at home when she's overcrowded, when she hasn't got her own room?

Of course, if you've got company or somebody comes late of an evening and stays late, I won't let them go to bed because I don't want other people to see how they are sleeping. It's embarrassing, you see, a girl of her age. It's embarrassing for the boy as well, with his friends.

They told me at the school that the boy was doing wonderful and he had a marvellous brain on him. His tutor told me that no matter what O level or A level he was to go in for he could possibly pass. But the thing is he can't study of a night because there's nowhere for him to study. The twins are here, and we're here. He needs that room on his own to study – which he can't do. Owing to this he can't go to bed to the last minute, he doesn't get enough rest. The teacher said he is losing his education over this.

The twins play with a little girl of six who lives in the Towers across the road. She was up here the other evening and she wanted to go to the toilet. When I took her down to the toilet she refused to go in it. I felt really humiliated. I felt terrible about it. To think that my children have got to use the toilet – and they've had it for five years since they were born. Yet other children have never had it because they've always lived in nice surroundings. This little girl went back home to use the toilet. I felt terrible.

I can't let anyone in. For, of a Saturday or Sunday, my girl likes to lay in. I've got to keep the door shut, because of them coming in and seeing my daughter in bed. She's sixteen. She doesn't want people walking in. It's very embarrassing. Sometimes the wind blows the door open when I'm cooking. I have to keep the door and the window open for the heat in here. You might get somebody come up, knock on the door and just put their head round, like they usually do during the week when I'm here. And I have to say, 'Not yet. She's still in bed.'

You know, it's so awkward, because her room is next to the door to the stairs. My husband and I are in the room away from the door. It wouldn't be so bad if it was me and my husband on our own. It would be luxury, really. But this way it isn't, you see. There's nothing we can do. It isn't big enough to partition off.

We've no bath. We've only got cold water. And we have to go down to the sink every time we want cold water. If you was to be here bath nights you'd have a fit. It's such a commotion it takes me about three hours. I don't know if you saw the polythene bath I've got in there. It's the baby's bath really, but we can't get anything bigger, because we haven't got the room. So first of all I go downstairs to the sink and I bring up half a bath of cold water, and I put the kettle and all the pots on the stove for the hot water. Then I fill up and I wash Karen's hair. Then I do the same thing again and I wash Mona's hair. Then I do the same thing again and I wash the baby's hair. Then I've got it another three times with the bathing. I bring it up again.

Then there's getting the hot water. I must use three shillings or four shillings worth of gas on pots and kettles, just to bath them alone. I have to carry the water down the stairs to empty it and up again with clean water. If my husband's not here I've got to do that and I'm whacked out. I used to have an hour's rest before I finished the third one off. Whereas if you had got a bath they could soak in it together. You can't in a small bath because of the dirt that comes off the children.

There's four families on one floor that use this one tap and the toilet. There's a single man in that room there, and a single room in that flat there. Then there's a single man in that room, and he's always got loads of friends in, which is natural for a young man of twenty. Naturally all his friends use the toilet, you know, as well as my family. So roughly, on a Saturday, when he's got his friends in, there must be fifteen or sixteen people in and out of the toilet all day. They are not noisy people, but naturally they have a few beers. So they're going all the time to the toilet. Every time I want to go down to the toilet, or my husband, or the twins, there's usually somebody in it. You've got to wait. And nobody likes going to a toilet when somebody's just come out. I have to buy Dettol and toilet rolls. I have to carry them down as I go down, because, naturally, if they're down there other people are going to use them. I'd be going through four or five bottles of Dettol a week. So that's very inconvenient.

Then I've got a young cousin that lives upstairs. She hasn't got any children. So naturally they come in late, and they giggle and laugh up the stairs. You can't tell people to keep quiet. They are not doing it intentionally. But sometimes she brings friends in for a cup of tea, and they run up and down to the toilet, you know. So you've got the noise. If the baby slept in here she'd get no sleep at all. I was going to bring her in here when she was ill, because of us all breathing in one room, but we couldn't, because there are so many families living in the house they are continually running up and down the stairs all the time.

My husband has spent an awful lot of money on this place, a fortune practically. Tiling the ceilings. He had to plaster all this wall before he could paper it or paint. And he's put in all the tiles over by the cooker, because of the steam and the dirt and the grease. It's easy to wash down. The thing is, if you do go into a council place then you can make it something and you are working for something.

I've got all this furniture in here – and it's good furniture. It looks nothing because it's in horrible surroundings. You've got a cooker and a fridge in the same room as the suite. You can't make it look anything. It's all crowded in.

I haven't got any more room in our bedroom, so as to change the furniture round. Therefore the only way I can fit it in is by putting the dressing table completely up against the wardrobe. A lot of people would think I should get rid of the dressing table, but I need it for the drawers, to put the clothing in. Therefore it's completely up against one door of the wardrobe. So you can only open one, you can only use one. So everything is jammed in and when you get anything out I've got to re-iron it again. It takes all my patience ironing a thing. Then I've got to iron it again before I can wear it.

We have tried to find somewhere else, but you just can't save with five children. They always want shoes or the boy's school uniform. When we have applied for a house they've wanted £150 down as a sort of key money. That's what they want. And we just can't do it. Then again, even if we had the key money, they don't want you with five children, especially three little ones. They just can't be bothered with young children now. So that's the finish of it.

We have been down to the Council a few times about the over-crowding and they say they can't put us any further forward on the list than they have done. When we did go to the Town Hall in Marylebone Road about two years ago we asked them about a flat, and he said to me, 'Four-bedroom flats are very hard to find. But if you hear about one going notify us and we'll see what we can do about it.' Which I did. Every time I went down about one they said it had been allocated to somebody. So we're just hoping they will bring the house down so that then we will be rehoused.

The thing is, I'd have to go out to work full-time to earn the rent. But you'd know you were working for something. Here you are working for nothing.

PHILIP FENDER: *Emigrating*

Philip Fender is a skilled man, working for the Post Office, helping to instal new exchanges. A member of the Post Office Engineering Union, he brings home, net, about £25 a week. He lives in a ground floor tenement in the same street.

I went into the Brigade of Guards as a National Serviceman. I did three years in the Guards. I came out, I met the wife, and we got married. I moved into a flat in Kilburn. We lived there for ten years and we had our name down on the Council all the ten years. And still nothing was done. The place was damp. In the end the landlord did the place up, but he didn't do the roof. The water was still coming in and we were still getting dampness.

I had a chance to move into here just over two years ago, so I took it. It hadn't been decorated for thirty years, because there had been an old person living in here. I did all the place up myself, and all the walls. And then we got the same trouble here – dampness on the kitchen wall. The window sashes had gone.

So I decided to emigrate. I'm emigrating out to South Africa. I've got a job out there, and an unfurnished flat, and that's near enough why I'm going. There are plenty of unfurnished flats out there at £10 a week.

I've got two children: Stewart, he's aged six now. He's had a lot of colds and chest complaints, you know. He's had his adenoids and tonsils done, because the doctor thought they should be done. It's made a little bit of difference, but he still gets the colds and the coughs. The little girl, Jackie, is eight, she's a good girl, you know. Her health has been a bit dodgy, colds and that. I'm sure it's through the dampness. My wife – she's quite fit. She's had a few colds, and I suffer from chest myself, from bronchitis.

I've served my country and I think it wouldn't hurt the country to do *me* some favours. I was on active service out in Cyprus – the same as it is in Northern Ireland at the moment, the same trouble. I thought naturally that since I was born and bred in Great Britain that they could provide a house, a council place with a little garden, so I could bring my children up as children should be brought up.

They have to play out in the street now. It's very dodgy out in the street, what with the traffic. My little boy, he's going through the stage now when he wants to play soldiers. He loves playing – and I'd have liked to have him playing in a little garden. Where I am going to emigrate there will be a little garden.

JIM KELLY: *Mice in the children's bed*

Jim Kelly lives on the ground floor in the same block of tenements. He is the secretary of the newly-formed tenants' association. Big, burly and determined looking, he is thirty, and has been a railwayman. Having spent the morning looking for a job, he is eating his mid-day meal with his wife. She is younger. With three young children cramped in the two rooms of her home, she has her hands full – and looks it.

One Sunday we went out for dinner. We arrived back about half past six. The dustbins were in the passage outside our front door.

We looked out of the back and there was anything up to six inches of raw sewage floating in the backyard and into the back of the flat.

After some panic we managed to get the Council people round here to clear it. We finished sweeping what was left after it had gone down the drains.

Whilst the builders were clearing out the backyard a nest of rats was found. We held on to these until somebody came down. Unfortunately they couldn't come, so we destroyed 'em. I found mice in the children's bed. Then we had a cat, and he caught seven mice in the first week.

The baby is nearly a year old. I don't think she has had a month in which she has had good health – there's always been something wrong with her. All the family has had gastro-enteritis or gastric 'flu. If one gets it they all get it. One has chronic bronchitis. This can only be put down to the damp, which is very evident in all the rooms. It's getting worse and worse, all the time.

The structure is supposed to be sound, according to all reports. But we know better: it's not sound. My toilet is coming down. The overflow from the floor above is coming into our toilet. I have to put newspapers down to soak it up.

Any movement above us is amplified. It's just like living under a herd of elephants.

I'd like to get out of London altogether. I start work at the Post Office very shortly. If I can make a success of this job, after a year I will put down for a transfer to one of the new towns or developing towns. This, I think, would help both our physical and mental state of health.

I did write to one firm about buying our own house. I got a nice brochure back, showing all the houses. The one we were interested in was about £5,000. Two letters came with it, explaining the mortgage arrangements. Before I could be considered for a mortgage I had to earn more a week than I am earning, and you had to put down a certain deposit.

Mrs Kelly: The wiring is so bad in this flat we can't have a washing machine or anything, because it fuses all the time. It blows. I've been told it's dangerous. I was told it would cost £90 to rewire the flat. That was six years ago. How much it would cost now I don't know. When I first moved in I was told that all repairs was my responsibility.

We've three children. It's not so easy for me. The children can't go out to play unless they are in the street or round at my mother's. The young one, who is two, usually runs away. So I have to go searching. They can't really play indoors because they have only got the bedroom to play in. And with five beds in it – or four I should say – they can't really play in there. It's getting me down with all this at the moment. So I have to be on the doctor's list for tablets for my nerves.

One day the two-year-old, the little boy, got lost. He ended up down St Mary's Terrace, which is on the way to the canal. He ended up by being picked up by a policeman and being taken down to the police station. It's worrying because of the canal – they can get in there easily – and it does frighten me. He has to be let out because I don't think it's nice to stay in these places. He sees other kiddies playing out, and so he wants to play out, which is only reasonable. Any child would. All the time I'm on nerves. Even when I have to go to work I'm still nervous, because this particular incident happened when I was at work. Someone else had the worry of it, which I don't think is fair. But I'm still worried anyway.

I'm out to work to try and save some money for when we are moving. Not only that, it helps my state of mind to get out of these sort of places at least for five nights a week. Otherwise I think I would be a mental wreck, which the doctor told me. I'm the manageress of a bar. My mother has the children.

Jim: There's no bath in our house. All the houses in our street haven't got a bath. We ourselves use a bungalow bath – the old tin bath, which we bring in here in the kitchen. We boil plenty of kettles and things like that which hold water, bath the kids, empty it out by a bowl into the sink, and then hang it out again, which takes about an hour and a half altogether. There's no hot water, no geyser. The only method of getting hot water is by using a kettle or a saucepan on the stove. It's a slow business, but there you are. We are living in old flats so we have to use old methods.

There was an accident the other day. On the front of these houses there's a bit of artistic masonry, which just happened to fall off the wall from a height of fifteen or twenty feet. Fortunately there was no-one under it at the time. It could have caused very serious damage.

We had to attend a meeting of the Council the week after it

happened, and this masonry was produced as evidence of our plight in the council chamber by one of the councillors who were fighting for our case.

Since we had the the council meeting when this street was first mentioned a few of us who are interested have got together – mostly the younger ones – and we are in the process of forming a tenants' association. We've had a lot of sympathy from other councillors, who have said they will come and talk to us at our meetings.

BETTY HOOPER: *Damp and overcrowded*

A top floor flat – again in 'Rachman Road' – with everything tucked away to provide living space. The tablecloth is clean and there is fresh paint everywhere. Mrs Hooper keeps her home bright and spotless, as she does her children. But her voice contrasts with the spirited and determined effort she is clearly making to provide a proper home for her family. She speaks in a dull, lifeless voice, as if she has had to accept bad housing conditions for too long.

We've been here eight years. We all sleep in the same room, that's two children and me and my husband. We rewired the flat ourselves – and we're still waiting to be repaid by the landlord. We've put in our own toilet and we've done it all up, because it was in a terrible state when we moved in.

We've also got damp. The windows are in danger of falling out of the bedroom into the street. We put our own Ascot in for our hot water. I go to my mother's for a bath. We bath the children in the bowl.

We did have an offer of a council flat. It was too high – £9 10s a week, which we can't afford. We'd like a council house – but it's the rent problem. If the rent's too high it's no good. Also we live right at the top and I have to keep going up and down stairs to see to the children in the street. They are always calling up: they want to go to the toilet. I'm everlasting up and down.

Also, when they was babies, I had to carry them up the four floors with the pram, you know. There's nowhere for them to play indoors. They get on your nerves when they're stuck in. If they go up and down the stairs people in the house complain when the door is left open downstairs on to the street. And they complain about the children leaving the toys in the passage, because they've got a bike and a pram. You can't keep on going up and downstairs with a big pram all the time.

We pay £2.89 a week rent, plus £30 a year rates. I think it's very bad the way the rates keep going up for this place. I think they are a bit high, considering my brother, who's got his own house and doesn't pay as much as we do in rates.

We have thought of trying to buy our own house. We got in touch with the Greater London Council to get a mortgage, but they didn't want to know, because they said we are not being evicted, so we don't stand very much chance. If we was being evicted perhaps they would consider it – a hundred per cent mortgage. Unless we got a hundred per cent mortgage we couldn't afford it. My husband is a sheet metal worker, earning £30 a week. On my husband's bring-home wage of £25 a week we couldn't save. That means I'd have to go out to work and that means I'd have to leave the children, which I wouldn't do.

If we did get an offer of a flat at £9 10s a week they said we would get a rebate, which would only be about a pound off. We still couldn't afford £8 10s a week, which is a third of my husband's wages. That means that by the time he has given me my money for food we wouldn't have no clothes to wear.

There was an old couple used to live next door. His wife used to suffer from bronchitis caused, I think, by the flat being so damp. We've been here nearly eight years, and her ceiling was down when we moved here, and they have never come to repair the ceiling. He put stays in the bedroom to keep the ceiling up. And now her husband is in hospital, very ill. She died of the chest trouble. First of all he suffered from bronchitis too, but now I don't think he will be coming out of hospital.

We did go on holiday last week – only to Maidenhead. I didn't want to come home, coming back to this place. We was looking at houses which were really nice, but which we could never afford, about £25,000. We was only living in a caravan, but it was still nice – nice to get away from here.

9. MP against the landlords

ARTHUR LATHAM

*Arthur Latham is the hardworking Labour MP for North Paddington.
At the three advice bureaux he holds regularly in the different parts of
the constituency housing cases outnumber all the rest put together.*

*He has sponsored an organisation called 'Help Expose Lousy Land-
lords,' – HELL for short. When dealing with Government Ministers,
the Westminster City Council or landlords, if he sees that he is receiving
little response, the MP finds that publicity about the evils of delays in
the local and national press and on television can sometimes get results
which could be achieved in no other way.*

*Having been Chairman of the Housing Committee on Romford
Borough Council for a number of years before becoming an MP Arthur
Latham is conversant with the problems of local authorities and the
financial, legal and technical intricacies involved.*

*When not engaged in the Chamber or committee rooms Arthur
Latham works in his small office on the upper corridor of the House of
Commons, overlooking the Thames. It contains an MP's standard
equipment: typewriter, telephone, desk, filing cabinet and bulging
briefcase. These are the tools he uses to cope with the ceaseless flow of
correspondence.*

Over ninety-five per cent of the property in Paddington is rented.
One can find all types of tenancies within the constituency. The
Greater London Council has properties with rents of about £8 to
£9. Westminster City Council has similar rent levels. The Church
Commissioners own a considerable number of properties. In
addition, the Mulberry Housing Trust has bought up a good many
properties and modernised them floor by floor, not to local authority
standards but to a reasonable level of conversion. There is also the
old Queen's Park estate, which was built for what were then known
as 'uniformed' tenants – railwaymen, postmen and policemen. A
large number of these have now been taken over by the Westminster

City Council, which has a limited, long-term, unambitious improvement programme to replace outside toilets with a bath and inside toilet at the expense of one bedroom. Some of them are being demolished.

Beyond that there are many three-storey properties, which, together with attics and basements, provide landlords with an opportunity for five individual lettings. From the experience of HELL we have ascertained that an average of about £6 a week for poorly furnished accommodation is being charged, in many cases with bathrooms and toilets being shared. Often individual bathrooms are provided but are not in fact available because they are in an unusable state of repair.

The Westminster City Council claimed about a year ago there had not been a great increase in the incidence of furnished properties. This is quite contrary to the evidence we have been collecting. Because what now happens is that, as soon as an unfurnished floor becomes vacant, the landlord will step in, put in the minimum of furniture and then let it as a furnished dwelling. This has two advantages from the landlord's point of view. First of all he circumvents all the Rent Act legislation applying to unfurnished dwellings. He can get his tenants evicted very easily within a month. Beyond that he can obtain much higher rents than he would be allowed to do for unfurnished dwellings.

The properties themselves do not provide tenants with privacy. There are some cases of appalling landlords who deliberately neglect the dwellings for which they are responsible. Even those where the landlords are relatively 'good' the living conditions in which people are being expected to raise families are far from any reasonable standard. The prospects for people living in such accommodation – usually overcrowded – of getting any alternative is very remote. The Westminster City Council housing list stands at 6,000. People wait years for alternative accommodation. Many of those people about whom we are speaking would find it impossible to pay the rents charged for modern council property suitable to their needs.

Multi-occupied properties present a particular problem because, apart from the four major landlords I have mentioned, the houses which are let floor by floor are owned by a multiplicity of landlords, sometimes owning two or three properties, sometimes only one. There is a further complication in that it is extremely difficult at times to discover who is the particular landlord on whom responsibility should be pinned for neglect, dilapidations generally and lack of necessary repairs.

The Church Commissioners have a strange practice, too, of acting as the ground rent landlord and letting to a second person who, in a number of cases, lets to a third party, and sometimes even to a fourth party. Not only is the tenant confused as to who is the landlord, but I have found that even the local authority is in considerable difficulty in discovering who to serve with statutory notices to get urgent repairs attended to. There is the problem of identifying the particular landlord.

Now the people in ownership of the properties are sometimes people of long standing. Others are those who have bought a multi-occupied property with sitting tenants, when one unfurnished floor became vacant, in order to provide accommodation for themselves. Some of the landlords operate in several parts of London, and the difficulty is in building up information about the deliberately neglectful habits of a particular landlord. Furthermore, we have a number of cases where the landlord, having collected maybe £1,500 a year rent from a single multi-occupied property, at the end of a five years period, will then sell that property either in the event of a floor becoming vacant or will try to sell it to a housing association. This association will then inherit the defects and dilapidations, whilst the landlord pockets the difference. The sad thing is that, if one rules humanity out, this is good business for some of the landlords. Because if he has £1,500 a year coming in for five years, without spending on repairs, and then sells the property, he can recoup his original outlay with a pretty substantial margin remaining.

It is this commercial aspect of housing exploitation within the constituency which I think presents the greatest difficulty. At the moment it is profitable for landlords to neglect their property and sell it at the end of a short period of ownership.

There are a number of instances of harassment, not quite on the scale of what was called Rachmanism. We don't get alsatian dogs used, but you get noisy tenants moved in above a quiet tenant. There have been attempts to evict tenants illegally by giving them notice to quit. There have been cases of forcible entry.

One of the weaknesses in the legislation covering harassment, of course, is that it has to be proved to be deliberate and persistent. The number of prosecutions brought by the Westminster City

Council is below twenty. Yet the number of cases we have come across is considerably in excess of that. The harassment officer himself knows of more cases than that but fears that he hasn't got the necessary evidence to bring about the prosecution. Of course the motive is to get rid of a controlled tenant or simply to get rid of a tenant because there is another tenant waiting who is prepared to pay considerably more.

Whilst it is true that the tenant may apply for a registered rent, there are two deterrents to that. One is that the tenant will have no security having had the rent registered. So there is an element of fear which prevents him from taking the necessary action. The second is simply that tenants remain unaware of their rights. Housing is desperately short in the area, and if they can get a property for ten or twelve guineas, however poor the conditions, they will accept it and put up with the conditions, rather than have no roof over their heads.

The Westminster City Council has the North Westminster project, which is a great planner's dream, which may take ten years or more to complete, by which time a generation of children will have grown up. The plans look very nice. The action taken is very little in evidence so far. They have also circulated the landlords of old properties to accept the improvement grants. Of course there is no compulsion about this and the landlords have little motive to accept them. They don't mind so long as they are collecting their rent. Since so many of them are quite prepared to sell the property after five years of neglect, they have no incentive at all to improve. So far as rents are concerned, they can collect all they can extort at the moment. On the last report we had, the number of landlords responding to the City Council's proposals had been less than one per cent.

I believe there is a need for action, not only in North Paddington, but in London as a whole. Particularly in the neighbouring borough of Brent, the Royal Boroughs of Kensington and Chelsea, which also have some very poor property, and throughout most of the inner-London area where you will find not all of the problems of North Paddington, but very similar ones.

What can be done about it? I think the only adequate answer to this is a new public housing authority that will take over properties from landlords, not hamstringing itself with compensation based on the inflated 'fair rents' that are being registered, but taking it over on a financial basis related to the initial cost of building and the income that past owners have received from it. And then to set about modernising those properties at a level of rents which working class people can afford. The most appalling comparison at the moment is with new council property at Lisson Green, where the economic rents before subsidy are said to be in excess of £19 a week. Already the rents being charged are more than half the tenants' incomes in many cases.

Unless there is some massive public intervention of that kind, with the necessary financial support from the Exchequer, what will happen is that ordinary working-class families will be crushed right out of central London. We shall have luxury apartments at premium rents, and the ordinary working families who have generations of roots in the area will be forced out of the district altogether.

. . . in Glasgow

10. In the tenements

BESSIE REID · DONALD KIRKWOOD · HELEN MEACHER

BESSIE REID: *'The rats are terrible'*

She is only forty-nine, but years of living in terrible conditions make her seem twenty years older. All her teeth are out, and presumably she is waiting for false ones. Her face is thin and worn, with a sharp, pointed chin.

You come in to her Gorbals tenement through a dark, rotting, filthy entry. Then you climb up four flights of stone steps, worn away by generations. You pass the communal toilets, each serving three families. There is gas lighting on the landings, but in some of the toilets there is complete blackness. Mrs Reid strikes a match to show a hole in the wooden floor of the lavatory, about six inches square, which has been gnawed out by the rats. She has stuffed it up with newspaper.

'The children are frightened to go in there,' she says.

I'm twenty year in this house. I've five children in here. My husband is dead. We've two bedrooms and a kitchen. The rats are terrible. I could show you woollen jumpers that have been ate away with them. The kids are afeared to go to sleep at night because of them. You've got to keep the light on.

No bath. No hot water. You just have to boil a kettle on the gas. The three oldest can go to the hot baths. Well, that's two shillings a time. If you are bathing the two young ones you need four kettles of hot water each.

My name was down on the council waiting list first nineteen year ago. When my husband died I went to get everything changed into my own name. Everything was mislaid. They couldn't find the name, so I had to get everything re-registered. It was the rats that got me there. I showed them the two woollen jumpers ate away with the rats.

I'm going to go to a four-room apartment with a bathroom. It's something to look forward to. I pay £4 a month. But I'll have to pay £16.70. I've put in for the rent rebate, but I don't know if I'll get it or not. Because at present I get £11.90 family allowances and widow's pension altogether. The eldest boy is seventeen and isn't working. He gets £3. He was an apprentice plumber but he was made redundant. It's difficult to get a job. In fact he went down in London for three months. And that's him back up. He couldn't get a job anywhere.

It'll be a better upbringing for the children in the new house. Plenty of space and hot water. The children had only the back court to play in. It's like a quagmire, a mud patch. The garbage was put there, and the children were playing in it. There's no facilities here.

There are fields where they are going, if they are allowed to play in them. It's out in the country, on the outskirts. I don't mind moving – not if it improves their chances. It's bound to be healthier out there. I'd want to be out of this place altogether, for the sake of the kids. Though the bus fares will be ninepence each way if the boy comes to work in the centre. Financially I'll be worse off. The removal firms want £14.50, but the Social Security only gave me a grant of £2.75.

My husband had medical priority, because he had cancer. He lay on that bed for two solid years. I had to carry him down the stairs onto the landing to the toilet. On top of that I had to bring up the family. If he'd been able to get a low down house in the country I'm certain it would – at any rate – have helped him along during the misery he was suffering. And he had no privacy. He had no privacy at all. He was stuck in that room with the kids running in and out. I mean you're bathing him and you're chasing the kids out. They're not doing me a favour in giving me a house. No. When it would have been a real amenity for me I couldn't get it.

Mr Kenny from down below has done up the furniture and painted it for me so it will be nice when I move into the new house. I'll have to buy carpeting and extra beds. I'll get it on HP I suppose.

5

DONALD KIRKWOOD: *The curse of low wages*

A third-storey tenement south of the Clyde. It is shared by two families: those of Donald Kirkwood and his married daughter, Helen. Both families have been forced back into the slums by low wages. To reach the close, or entry as it would be called in England, you walk across a quagmire. The mud and stagnant pools are all the children have for a playground. The windows on the staircase are broken. The obvious disrepair confirms the Kirkwoods' complaint, 'They do no repairs for us at all.' However, their flat has a new door – Donald Kirkwood has constructed it himself. He is a slightly-built, smiling, friendly man, but in repose his face is marked with lines of anxiety.

I'm forty-three years of age with six children. I'm a widower but I'm remarrying. I come from the Gorbals originally, born and bred here. This building here will be ninety or a hundred years old. My home consists of three apartments, what they call two rooms and a kitchen. Two bedrooms and one kitchen. There's no kitchenette, as you can see. There's an inside toilet but no bath. You don't have hot water unless you want to have a geyser. It's not laid on for you. We're three storeys up.

I'm a driver for a haulage contractor. Overtime we don't get now because things are so bad in the haulage. I get £18.50 gross, or about £16 to take home after stoppages. If I do get overtime I take home about £20.

At one time I had a Corporation house – that was when I had two children. Then I had another four children, and the rents were so high I was in difficulty. The rent was three pounds a week and, after stoppages, I was only earning ten and a half pounds a week at that time. Naturally my wife couldn't go out to work, because of the young children. At that time there was none of the children earning. They were all at school. So I had to look out for a cheaper house. So I came down to the South side. That was six years ago.

After my wife died it was even worse. We were so far away from the relations and people, old neighbours who would give you a bit of help in a situation like that. But the main factor was finance. Rather than have the children taken away I kept them together. It was pretty hard trying to run the home and work at the same time.

Up there I couldn't do it, but round here I could because there are so many neighbours I know. My wife's people and my own people were round here.

There were terrible disadvantages in leaving a modern house, because the children had a bathroom and a bit of a garden. They can only play in the streets here. Some of the houses round here will be standing another ten or twelve years. This one will be standing another three years.

The main disadvantage about this house is that it's so small, and you don't have a bath in the house. You have to go to the public baths. It's not real healthy. These wee rooms are damp. You can see the damp in the walls. There's nothing you can do about it, it's so old. The factor (agent) has tried and tried. We pay six pounds per month rent.

HELEN MEACHER: *Forced back into the tenements*

Helen Meacher – Donald's daughter – looks about sixteen. In fact she is twenty-three. Close cut chestnut hair, demure, quiet. More like a schoolgirl than a mother. Nursing a baby as she talks. Her husband's troubles, like her father's stem mainly from the low wages.

Both families have had to leave Corporation houses and return to old slum tenements.

My husband earns £16 take home pay. It's about £18, I think, before stoppages. He works in a tea warehouse. We've been married nearly two years. The baby is called Diana. The house I used to live in before I got married was a condemned house. It's down now. There were eight of us living in it, with three bedrooms and a kitchen. You had no room to wash. You only had a wee sink – just like the one we've got here. Anything you wanted to wash you had to pay for in the launderette. You couldn't get anything washed or dried at home.

When we got married I went to live in another old house, just a room and kitchen. Just like this, but with only one bedroom. We got a new council house. But now I'm back here. We couldn't afford the new one. The rent was £13.60, but in Glasgow at the end of the year everybody had to pay an increase in rates, which meant £17 for us to pay in back rates, even though we hadn't been in the house for many months.

Peter is twenty-two. He's been in the tea warehouse for about six years on and off. He blends the tea. It's just a wee firm. In the summer he goes into the building trade you know. Then he get's overtime. But he doesn't get any overtime in the warehouse.

When your house is being condemned they ask you to fill up a form saying where you would like to live and what size house. I said that for a small family like ours a bedroom and a kitchen and a living-room would be big enough. But when I went down they told me I was getting a three-bedroom house at Thornley Bank, away on the outskirts. I said I didna ask for that. And he says to me, 'You don't think you get what you ask for.' So I said, 'Then why did you bother asking in the first place?' But he said I wasna long enough on the Corporation list.

By the time you have paid the coal and your electricity and maybe your insurance, you had nothing left by the time you fed yourself and put the rent away. You wouldn't have anything extra for something you didn't know you would have to spend. We had an electric cooker. I think the electricity would cost about £20 a quarter. And that was without the coal fire.

I didn't ask for a rent allowance. I didn't know anything about that.

Peter, her husband: There's mice in all these old houses. We're overrun with them. The rats are outside. Open the window and you can see them. When you're cooking the smell's all over the place. It's a kitchenette and a sitting-room all in one.

Helen: The baby's not so well. Just now I've got two bottles: a bottle of penicillin and a bottle for her catarrh. And drops for her eyes. I went to the doctor's with her yesterday. It's just next door. And this is what the doctor said when I went in: 'What a place this is. It's no wonder she's full of catarrh. And she has an infection of the eye.'

I left her one time in the pram at the bottom of the stairs. It was only for a second. I was up the stairs as I had my washing. When I came back to the pram there was two cats in it. It was the smell

of the milk that drew them. You couldn't leave your baby there.
The baby's got a go-chair that folds up. I can get it up the stairs.
But when I had a pram and had to get her up three stairs as well
I used to have to leave her in her cot. Then I'd have to go down
with the pram and then run back and get her. If I went a message
I'd have to leave the pram till night time when my husband came
off his work. There was one time – she was only about four weeks
– I left the pram and brought the baby up. When I went down again
the blankets and everything were away. Someone had taken them.

Peter: We'd very much like a council house if the wages were
better. What I'm getting is the average wage in Scotland for a
labourer.

Helen: I'm working myself just now, part-time, you know. It's just
a Saturday and a Monday. On Saturday my husband watches the
baby and on Monday my mother does. We've been trying to save
for a deposit on a house. On Friday I went to a few places. I went
to a factor and he gave me the keys for a house. A house like this,
but with just a room and kitchen. It was £850, a hundred pounds
deposit. And the kitchen wasn't even a room like this. There wasn't
even a hall. You just opened the door and you were in the kitchen.
No toilet. Four families sharing the outside toilet.
    We're trying to save up for a deposit. It's not so bad now because
I've got that part-time job. Saturday from half eight in the morning
till nine at night and a Monday from half eight to half five at
Littlewood's pools. You get nearly £8 for that. So that I'm getting
more than my husband's rate. I don't know how long it will take us
to save the hundred pounds.

A neighbour: You see how prices are rocketing even for old tenement properties. Helen told you that it's £850 for a room and
kitchen, with an outside toilet. The value of that house is only
about £200. It's not worth that. But £850 is the kind of prices they
fetch. Now these proprietors and house factors know about high
rents, they don't mind asking these prices. And they'll sell the
houses. Because people will put down a deposit of, say, £50 and
then pay about fifty shillings a week over a length of time, whereas
they would have to pay £17 or £20 a month rent for a council
house. This is the reason they are buying these old houses. Before

they even get the houses paid for they will be condemned. So they'll be back to Square A. They wouldn't get full compensation for the house. The assessor comes round and values it. They'll get the value that he fixes on it – maybe half what they paid for it. There should be a control placed on the value that these houses sell at.

This new rents Bill just suits the house factors and the private landlords. It will be cheaper to stay in a house and room than in a council house. The private owners and factors can ask almost any price they like.

Her father: Just look at this room. I'd say it was ten foot by eight. No more. You live, cook, eat, watch the television, everything in the one room.

Helen: You'll see notices in the *Times* every Tuesday and Thursday night saying, 'We buy or sell houses. We'll give you cash prices.' So maybe you can sell for £300 or £400 and they'll put them on the market at £750. Just a room and kitchen or single ends. Houses built ninety or a hundred years ago, houses that we've been fighting in the Gorbals to get the sanitary officers and Medical Officers of Health to have condemned. Because they are inadequate, the cause of ill-health and TB. Instead of going forward we seem to be going back. Some are getting a good job and a fair wage, though they are working hard for it. If a man's getting over £20 a week he's doing overtime. But there aren't many men in Scotland today coming out with over £20 a week who aren't doing two or three hours' overtime. Where they get their average wage figures from I don't know. One of the biggest sinners are the local authority themselves. Take this point of washing. The damp clothes have got to hang inside the house, and that's unhealthy. There's no facilities for washing. You have to dry the clothes by the fire. I've got nappies all round. You can go to the launderette, but it costs you plenty, you know. Once a week I go to the launderette, but I couldna go with nappies.

11. Rehoused in the country

ELSPETH STEWART · GWEN BATEMAN
PETER MCLINTOCK

Seventeen miles outside Glasgow, at Ladyton, where the beautiful Vale of Leven leads to Loch Lomond, there stand several housing estates built for the Corporation by the Scottish Special Housing Association. These are among the most modern, most attractively designed and best equipped houses in the country. In London they would have sold for over £12,000. They are maisonettes built in terraces, each with its own garden facing the river.

The SSHA is a publicly owned, non-profit making organisation set up by the Government during the war. It receives the same housing subsidy as local authorities.

ELSPETH STEWART: *'I'll never go back to Glasgow.'*

Mrs Stewart's house is in perfect array, though she herself has been interrupted in her housework (a headscarf partially covers the curlers in her hair). It is a dream house, thoughtfully designed, well built, and beautifully decorated. Built on three floors, it has a semi-open plan design. Every door is automatically sprung to lessen fire danger. There is a night storage heater providing off-peak heating. In the back garden there is a whirligig clothes drier, rotated by the wind.

Altogether a housewife's delight.

I'm forty-two this year. My husband and I lived in Glasgow for a great number of years. I thought the place was deteriorating. I really wanted to move out for the family's sake. It gives them more scope out here. I've teenagers and I've this other wee boy here to bring up. So it's a better environment. The old house was a

Corporation house, but it was damp. I felt I really liked a modern house.

In this house I have my own back and front entrance. With five apartments it's big enough for the family. They've got their own rooms and bring their own friends in and entertain them as they wish. It's a beautiful house. The rents are dear, but it's worth it. On the whole it's a really good house for the money.

My husband did all this decorating himself. He's a salesman-collector. He's quite handy with the decorating. I haven't put new furniture in yet. I had this furniture in my other home. All I needed was more bedroom furniture and a wee coffee table.

My first delight was my kitchen. It's spacious; we can all sit and dine in it. This leaves your sitting-room free – you don't have to set up a table. We usually eat in the kitchen because it's really a kitchen-dinette. It's a warm house – well insulated. I couldn't really find a fault in it. I'm really delighted with the house. I like the place also.

I've been here a year and five months, and I'd never go back to Glasgow, definitely not. I like space. We're not all closed in, on top of one another. There's a back and front garden. There's a big playing-field down there for the older boys who like to play football. The smaller children have other amenities.

The neighbours are friendly. They are just nice friendly people – not nosey friendly, just naturally friendly people, you know. I haven't been in any trouble, touch wood. But I quite believe that if you were in any trouble or if you were ill there would be somebody run to help you.

It's much quieter out here. Night time – after tea-time – it's very quiet. Even though they are big houses, family houses, it is quiet. I've five children myself, from nineteen down to three.

The three teenagers didn't quite take to it, the oldest girl especially. Not only that they lost their friends, but they found it was too quiet up here. There was nothing for them. My oldest girl wasn't a cinemagoer or a dancegoer, but she was a church member. She belonged to a Christian Endeavour Society, the Girl Guides and so forth. They do have these things up here. But it's difficult to take them away from the one place and get them started back in another group. They have managed it now. The oldest girl has a group of Girl Guides to look after, and she belongs to the

Youth Fellowship. She's out every night. And she still keeps in contact with her Glasgow friends. She goes twice a week.

The boy is happy at school. The other girl is beginning to settle now. But still she finds there's nothing to do at nights. She's different from the older girl. She wouldn't join any new clubs. If I said we were moving back to Glasgow I don't think they would really like to, because they have made new friends.

I like the country. My husband and I do quite a bit of walking when the weather permits it. We've been out to Balloch and Loch Lomond. I've actually walked to Balloch and back and enjoyed the scenery.

I'm a lot healthier since we came to live here. Maybe it's because I'm happier, less harassed. And this wee chap's been marvellous. The whole family is healthy as a matter of fact.

My husband works just outside of Glasgow. He travels from here to Clydebank by train. There's a half-hour service. I personally think it's worth the higher rents and the fares to be out here. I really do. My husband and I have worked it all out, and I still think we did a good thing in moving out when we got the chance. It's made a big, big, difference in my own personal life. I feel real settled and happy now. I don't think I could have got anywhere where I could be as contented as I am here. And I don't grudge my rent. The rents and rates are high in Glasgow, too. I feel myself getting on. I've been able to put bits and pieces in, and make it comfortable for the family. You can put your money into the houses and really see the result. They are dry and warm. My bill for the quarter's heating and lighting is about £35 to £40. And I'm not saying, 'put that off' or, 'turn that down'.

I suppose we are all different. Some people like being out in the open. Some people will sacrifice to get on a bit. And then there's others that just don't want to move.

You're about quarter of an hour's walk down to the shopping centre, but it takes you out. You'll never be stuck. There's always grocery and butchers' vans coming round. But twice a week I go into the town. I don't go into Glasgow much. I don't feel any inclination. The only time I went into Glasgow was to do some Christmas shopping. I have a sister in the heart of Glasgow, but she comes to visit us out here. She likes coming out. She says it's like coming on a holiday.

About a year and three months was all we waited for this house.

5*

We just kept phoning up to ask if houses were ready. They kept putting me off because I had a dog, just a wee children's pet, though I didn't realise that. They didn't want dogs because of all the open gardens. But there is quite a few dogs. They don't want too many. We got rid of our dog when I realised it was holding us back. My husband was upset at parting with the dog. But these are things you get over very quickly. I thought that children are more important than dogs.

Before we moved I was depressed and it was affecting the rest of the family. My husband and I get on much better now. I think that's because I feel more contented.

GWEN BATEMAN: *Getting together*

Mrs Gwen Bateman is the lively honorary secretary of the local tenants' association. She and her husband sit drinking tea in the bright kitchen, overlooking the fields at the back. He is a night worker, a printer on a daily newspaper.

In this part we've all come from Glasgow. I think most of us wanted to get away from the congestion, the hurly-burly, the old tenements, the outlook. Now they have a grand view here from the lovely big windows, a view of the Carman hills. There's a song about them. The fact is that they can look through their windows and have a bit of space in front of them. The children can play traffic-free, so mothers haven't the same worry about them. They also get a rest from the children. Then there's the health point of view. They've all got bathrooms now. Some even have two toilets. This is quite something for Glasgow people.

The community spirit has been good too, even though they were all strangers. The fact that they have all made this big step from the city has tended to bind them together. They are helping each other. We moved here nine months ago. I thought the spirit of neighbourliness here was really wonderful. It was like wartime over again. When my husband went out to dig the garden, in a few minutes there were three neighbours asking if they could help him.

This is something we are losing in the city both in the new estates there and also in the old parts. Very much so I would think. The spirit of keeping up with the Jones' has arisen – but not so much here. There seems to be a spirit of rejoicing in each other's happiness. I would say that we are all glad for each other. I found a feeling of gladness for each other, that we had got nice homes, nice outlooks and the children were having a better time.

Even the walk to the shops doesn't seem to be unduly worrying the young women. And now we are fortunate enough, we've got a bus service. This has been achieved through the tenants' association. And now we are nearly all getting a telephone service. We've got a public kiosk, and in a few weeks a fair number will be getting our own phones.

We are also very fortunate in the area. It's quite near an old town – Alexandria. They have accepted us, the newcomers. They don't regard us just as a set of Glasgow keelies (hooligans). So you get a combination of the old community and the new one. Unlike this estate, Livingstone and Cumbernauld are completely new towns, living on their own heart. But we have some of the old and some of the new, I think it's better to join in that way, particularly since they have accepted us.

We're of mixed ages on this estate: old, middle-aged and young. Some of the old people weren't very keen on having young children near them at first, particularly where they had lived previously in flats, where the children were always hanging round the door. But this has been smoothed out now. The tenants' association helped to do it. At the meetings the young parents explained how the children wanted their freedom. The old people explained the difficulties the children could cause. We arrived at greater tolerance by both sides. A councillor attends our meetings and gives us reports of what progress is being planned for the estate.

Parents came out here because they didn't want their children to become connected with vandalism. People came here who were prepared to sacrifice so that their children had a better life.

Her husband, Hector: Mind you, we are not wanting them to pull themselves out of their class, the working class.

Mrs Bateman: My brother emigrated to Canada. When I sent him photos of the country round our house he replied that if he had had this he wouldn't have emigrated.

PETER MCLINTOCK: *'It's marvellous – but . . .'*

He looks like an athlete, and in fact he must have been exceedingly fit to cycle thirty-four miles a day to and from work. Now, recovering from an operation, he sits back in his armchair, dressed in an open-necked sports shirt and flannel trousers. He has an emphatic style of speaking.

It has been marvellous for the children coming here. They've got more freedom. We've got four bedrooms, and they've got a room more or less to themselves. The boy has a room to himself. My girl has a room to herself. And I've got two girls in the other room. And we've got a baby about three months old. The children love it here. Marvellous. When we were living in the room and kitchen they were all stuck in the one room.

They've a lovely place to play. You can't run about on the grass, but there's plenty of room. There's not many cars to knock them down. We've got a wee maze over there for the kiddies to play in. And I dare say they'll build a swing park for them to play in. They've got a park across the way for children to play football It's really marvellous.

There are plenty of walks in the country. It's lovely fresh air. You can actually see Loch Lomond from the window.

My wife loves it She's got more space, she's got a drying green; a back and front door; a terrific lovely big kitchenette It's ideal for working in. We've a drying cupboard above the hot water tank.

As a builder I think the SSHA have made a very good job of these houses. There was just emulsion on the walls. I've papered this room myself. Well, yes, it is nicely furnished. I'm one of the lucky ones. I had bought the house we had in Glasgow. The money I got for that went in for furniture. Otherwise I'd just have the bare boards. I don't go in for hire purchase. If I've not got a thing I'll just have to go without.

You've got to get a better house to try and better yourself. It's no use staying in the slums in Glasgow in a room and kitchen. You can't get on. Your kids don't benefit from it. It's worth the sacrifice – only if they would stabilise the rent reasonable for a working man. If they would just understand the wage that's coming in after deductions. They don't realise that in the winter anyone in the building trade has a tight period. I've applied twice to the SSHA for a rent rebate, but they say I don't qualify. If you're earning £28 you're above it.

There's been a big change in the children's health. Bernadette was born with bronchitis. When she came down here she had her adenoids and tonsils out. That helped a lot. But the fresh air is definitely a benefit for them. They're out in all kinds of weather. They really like it down here.

We go out walking by Loch Lomond. I'm just off now for six weeks after a hernia operation. I usually get out during the day with the two small kids and the baby. Maybe we walk into Balloch. It's really lovely country.

Because they've got a room of their own they can put all their toys and all their books in that room. They are not interfered with. If they want to do a bit of studying when they get a bit older there'll be no one bothering them. You just learn them to keep the room tidy.

We've a bathroom and a small toilet downstairs. We've two toilets, really. If you're in the kitchen you don't have to run up to the top to go to the toilet, two floors up.

His wife: Before we had this we used to live in Glasgow in a single end. A single end is a one-room apartment, with a toilet outside on the landing. We got it when we were engaged, before we got married, so we could have some place to move into.

It's great here. It's great for the children. The children have far more freedom. You don't have to worry about their making a noise on top of people. Having a toilet and bathroom in the house makes a big difference. After we had the single end we bought a house in Glasgow with a toilet. That cost £112. That was very cheap. You see Peter done it up.

When we went for a house they offered us one at Easterhouse. It was more or less a rough district. We went out to see it. Gang slogans over the doors; all the windows painted. It was in a terrible condition. I said I wasn't taking it. I said I wanted a new house.

They said, 'there are priority cases. You'll just have to wait.' I said, 'Fair enough'. So I moved from that department to the overspill department. I put my name down for Cumbernauld or Dumbartonshire. I had to wait about a year. I think it was worth it.

In the old house it was a corner house. The stairs came down into the back court, into a well of the stairs. Everybody used to go down there and drink of a week-end, and leave bottles round there. And the dustbins were all full. There weren't enough facilities. They were getting emptied on the stairs, causing rats and vermin. We were dying to get out of it.

The cooking is easier here. You're not worried about the children running around the cooker, you know, in case they get burned. Where we were you just stepped out and you were on the main road – and that was you. You had always to see the children to the park every day. I'd be happy to stay here for many years. For ever, if we are allowed.

I think it's worth paying the extra for the advantages, though, to be honest, I didn't think the rents were going to be so steep. From fifteen guineas a month to go up to £22.40 is a bit high, when you've only one person's wage coming in.

Peter: We like it OK. But for a working man with five children the rents are that wee bit steep. Then there's the heating. We've been very fortunate with the central heating. We work it to suit ourselves. The wife and I have £21 to pay this quarter, because we've not been putting it on too much. In this type of house you're doing most of your work down in the kitchen. So this convector heater in the living-room doesn't get put on till we're coming back at about six o'clock. And we keep the water heater off during the night to save running up the bills. Next door the lady pays £23. And next door to her it's up to £30.

It's the rent, that's the real crippler. It's £22.40 per month. When we came down here sixteen months ago it was roughly £16. That's ideal. You can manage. But it's gone up twice, and they say it's going up again. If the Government puts the rent up there are three or four people round here saying they'll be moving. The working man can't afford this rent.

I'm a slater. If you ask for a rent rebate they want to know your basic wage – your wage without anything off. My basic on a normal week is about £28. That's for roughly 44 or 45 hours. The working week is 42½ hours. But by the time they deduct your tax, National Insurance graduated contributions, your stamps and all that, you're lucky to come out with £23 or £24. We don't get much overtime at present. The building trade is very slack. Our firm has been very slack. Just enough work to keep you going from day to day.

It's roughly seventeen miles from the centre of Glasgow. I've got to go there every day. I cycle in and cycle back, to save this wee bit of money. The train fare is just over £1.50. That's the return fare for a week. Well, I may sometime be sent to Hamilton, which is further. Granted I do get my expenses in that case. But you're just getting that money to cover ye. It's not bene-fiting you. So I usually save the train fare. I can manage to cycle it in an hour, each way, on top of a working day. Then I might get sent to Rutherglen, about four mile or so on the other side of Glasgow. So sometimes I do forty-two miles a day. But this is what you've got to do. You've got to try to get a wee bit by. It's just an existence. There's nothing you can put in the bank once you've paid your electricity and insurance and rent. There's only one wage coming into this house, you see. It's not so bad just now when the kids are small and you can pass clothes round about. But you think when they're teenagers, roughly eleven, twelve and thirteen. They're not working. There's no money coming in, and it's dearer then for clothes. We've got four family allowances. But that's only £3.90 or so. This has to be put by for buying clothes. When they get older they'll want pocket money for this and that. This is going to be the crunch.

12. The estates of Glasgow

HENRY ROBINSON · BELLA MCLINTOCK · JIMMY BELL
A GROUP OF MOTHERS

HENRY ROBINSON: *The caretaker's view*

Henry Robinson wears a black peaked cap, like a traffic warden's, bear-
ing the letters SSHA (Scottish Special Housing Association). Under
his black uniform coat he has on brown overalls. He is a tall, raw-boned
man in his forties. His own flat is in the centre of the estate. It goes with
the job, which he has held since the flats were built.

The two-bedroom flats are mostly for elderly people, and the
three-bedrooms are for family people with children. They've all
come out of old tenement houses. Generally speaking the tenants
do like the houses. They like the amenities, especially the bathrooms and the inside toilets. At the beginning they didn't like them
so much because they had been used to coal fires.

Some of them are still afraid to burn the electricity because of
the cost. Even though they use off-peak electricity they are
frightened to use it because of the price. Particularly the old folk.
It costs about £1.70 a week on average, for lighting, heating, cooking, the lot. That's a lot to come out of six pounds a week pension.
Their rent is covered by the social security supplement.

There seems to be a better community spirit here in these low-
rise flats than there is in the multi-storey flats. The majority of them
came from the same streets. They know one another. If strangers
come they make friends with them. They've only to meet once or
twice in the lifts – and that's it.

There's no amenities here for the children. Nothing. And that's
a most important thing. They should have a place of entertainment,
a hall of some description. In a community centre you could have a
special section for the older people. And I would put it under the
jurisdiction of the tenants' association.

My job is to help the people here if they get into difficulties with electrical faults, or I may have to release someone from the lifts. If anyone is seriously ill in the middle of the night somebody will come to my door and I can phone the ambulance.

The people here are conscious about keeping the buildings clean. They don't want them to be like the places they came from. Their main object in these flats is to keep things clean and tidy. But a very high proportion of the children has been before the courts. Though this environment is very good housing-wise, it's not very good social-wise. There's no picture house. The nearest is a sixpenny bus ride away. A community centre would help a lot.

There's nothing here for the teenagers. That's what's causing a lot of this vandalism. There's just a crowd hanging around the doors. And now – with so much unemployment – they can't afford to go anywhere. When they come out of school they don't get dole money. And what they get in social security wouldn't keep some of them in cigarettes and matches. They're hanging around doorways. The police come along, and they're booked for loitering. Having both parents out working is a big drawback, because the children need parental guidance. What they term the 'latch-key children' are having to let themselves into the house after school. Both parents are having to go out to work to earn enough to give them the amenities. When the parents get home they are too tired to be bothered with the children.

In many families they seem to get on together much better in the new homes. They all dig in: one will contribute a new carpet. Maybe the son will buy a television set; the mother will get something else. They have a real incentive in a new house. People moving into new houses are spending more time and more money in them.

BELLA McLINTOCK: *New flats, old problems*

The Gorbals area of Glasgow is not what it used to be. Vast numbers of the rotten old tenements have been demolished – though plenty remain. In their place stand all kinds of new council property: tower blocks, low-rise flats and two-storey houses. One huge eighteen-storey tower block – Queen Elizabeth Court – was designed by Sir Basil Spence.

Some of the inhabitants are critical of it, and it is known locally as
Alcatraz. A hundred yards away is the flat of Mrs Bella McLintock, a
grandmother. It looks fine. It is what many Glasgow families long for.
Even so Mrs McLintock expresses her dissatisfaction in sharp terms.

I was thirty-one years in that old top flat. I lived all that time with
the rain coming down on me. It was a smoke-filled house with a
big crack in the wall. We had to open the windows and the door
to let the smoke out. For thirty-one years I didn't have a dry
winter. The repair man came, but when he did it was just to shift
one slate from one part of the roof to another place where the rain
was coming down. Then he would walk away.

I'd got six children, living in two rooms and a kitchen. There was
eight of us there. I could cope with it. I had the three boys in one
bedroom; two girls in the other bedroom; and the baby was in a cot
in the kitchen along with the father and I. We had to use the kitchen.
We had mice but we kept traps and a cat to keep them down.

When I first got that house I went up to the Housing Department
and they told me they weren't taking any more names. That was
during the war. Then after eight or nine years I went up and put my
name down for a house. I waited for a house till a year ago. I put
down for this parish. I've three bedrooms. The rent when I came
in twelve months ago was £12 6s 8d a month. Then it rose to
£14 8s 9d. Now it's £16.75. And I've been told by people that's
well in the know of things that the Tory Government is going to
put up the rent another pound a week. That would mean £21 a
month. I don't think the house is worth it. The house is damp, in
the bedroom. We've got black mould in them. It comes through
the wallpaper. We've not redecorated since we came in because we
wanted to wait and see.

Last year we got flooded out in two of the rooms with water
coming in through the woodwork in the windows. Aye. Right
down the walls. These houses have been built about fourteen years.
I called the men out. They were supposed to repair it. But it's
coming in again. You leave a coat hanging in the wardrobe and it
gets all blue-moulded. I left my husband's suit over the back of
the chair and when we went to put it on him we couldn't put it on
him. He had been lying sick in bed at the time. I complained to the
Sanitary. I complained to the Health and Welfare. I complained
to the Social Security. The Social Security told me it was the

Corporation. Then the Corporation told me it was the Blind Welfare, because my husband is blind. I phoned the Blind Welfare again and they told me it was the Corporation. I sat down and wrote a letter to the Corporation. I got no reply. I wrote a letter to the Social Security. They came down. I showed them the clothes. They couldn't do nothing about it. So I wouldn't let them master me. We had to throw the clothes out.

The housing superintendent said it was caused by condensation. I don't think it is. I think in the building trade now they are not putting the building material into the housing. Twenty years from now the houses they are building will be slums. They tried to stop the damp. They pointed the windows outside. But still it's coming in. It's a wee bit better, but not much. Still damp.

My daughter got a new suite of furniture. When you pull out the drawers you can't get them in. The wood has swelled with damp-ness. We had to get the firm to take the thing away and file down the drawers so you could put them in. I see they are getting the same way again.

I had a girl of twenty-six here. The doctor thought her lungs was affected. He had her X-rayed. They said she had the cough but no spit. They X-rayed her again and it was clear. But they are still giving her tablets. The little grand-daughter who lives with us never used to get a cold till she came down here to live with us. This house is damper than the one we came from – even though there is no rain coming through the roof.

I think we should do what they are doing in Northern Ireland – hold back the rents.

Another thing is you can sit at your own fireside and hear the noise from your neighbours. From the floor above. They have children and they move the furniture up and down. We had to check them the other night.

JIMMY BELL: *Organising the tenants*

Jimmy Bell runs a small business in the Gorbals. Most of his time, how-ever, he devotes to helping the people with whom he grew up. Almost

everyone in the streets greets him with a friendly shout, and the old
people, the teenagers at the street corners, the housewives, the children,
they all know and like the fair-haired, broad-shouldered, man in his
thirties who tries to solve their problems.

There's a ward committee in every ward in Glasgow. It's non-
political. They are recognised as an official co-ordinating body;
they represent the tenants in putting forward complaints to the
Corporation; they do a good job. Each ward gets a £25 grant each
year to pay for the running expenses of the committee. Anything
to do with housing, drains, lighting or cleaning the streets can be
raised. If you feel you are in need of nursery schools or playgrounds
or community centres then we can write to the Town Clerk. In
turn the Town Clerk gives a copy of the letter from the secretary of
the ward committee to each councillor in that area. The department
concerned investigates, and a report is sent to the ward committee
and to the councillors. We can invite councillors to attend the ward
committee. It's quite a useful thing. Unfortunately the people
don't play an active part in it. And these committees are always
very small. But ours functions quite well. A secondary thing is that
we run an old folks' treat annually. Maybe we take 500 old folk down
to the coast for the day. We get the money from the public in the
bars and Bingo halls.

One of the problems in these flats was that at first they put old
age pensioners in the top flats. When the lifts broke down it was
not easy for the old people to walk up the stairs. Sometimes it can
be two days before they get a part for the lifts sent from England.
So now the old age pensioners won't take these high flats, but they
are still being offered them.

Mothers with young children don't like letting them out of the
door, because they don't know where they are. Whereas in the old
days they could look out of the windows and call to them.

This was a very densely populated area. It has been drastically
reduced, so a lot of families had to go to overspill. Over there is a
block of new flats which is still empty, because the people who were
to come to them found the rents would be too expensive. There
are actually some people who had homes there and who have
moved back into their old houses. The rents are £20 a month.
Then in October they will go up £1 a week under this new Tory
rent Bill. Every year after that they're going up ten shillings per

week. So this is going to cause a lot of overcrowding, because people just can't afford to pay for the houses. There's no use in building the houses if people can't manage to go into them. Housing is going to be run as a business rather than as a service for the people. To say that things will be solved by this Fizz (the Family Income Supplement) just won't do, because the grant they will get won't be sufficient to bring their wages up to the standard that they need. If they are going to put up the rent for a house of this size to £10 a week then they'll have to put the wages up as well.

A GROUP OF MOTHERS: *Run-down estate*

In the living-room of a young Catholic priest. The mothers are of mixed religions or of no religion at all. They have met there to discuss their housing problems, because there is nowhere else to meet. It is a sixteen-year-old Glasgow council estate. The houses are better than the rotten tenements most of the families originally came from. Yet there is widespread dissatisfaction with the lack of amenities and the way the estate is kept.

Mrs Jamieson: Well, I'm satisfied with this estate. I've got a bathroom, and an inside toilet, which I didn't have before. The air's cleaner.

Mrs McColl: But the place has deteriorated. I've been here thirteen years, almost since it started. I came from a poorer house too. It was a two-room and kitchen in the Gorbals. I was satisfied here for about eight years. I think it was until the vandalism, the houses being broken into. We live next to the school and it's being broken into two or three times a week. Though we've never been broken into in our house.

It's not just that there's nothing for the children to do. There's a lot for them to do if they are interested. There are Corporation youth clubs on this estate: football clubs, dance clubs, Boy Scouts, all connected with the schools.

Father O'Reilly: I would say that the school children are catered for, but those who have left school are not. A good thing would be some kind of fairly big sporting facility. It would need to have trained leaders.

A lot depends on the youth leader. If he has a fairly strong personality and the children feel safe it makes a big difference.

Mrs McColl: It's not just vandalism. In the last five years people don't seem to care about keeping their gardens. It's partly because a lot of gardens which *were* kept nicely have been spoiled by others. Then if your next door neighbour doesn't bother, you don't bother.

Mrs Collins: If the people up the stair or people walking in the street see kids doing any damage it would make a difference if they said something to the children.

Mrs Jackson: But if you say something it sometimes ends up that *you're* the one in trouble, because the parents come out and say it's none of your business. I've heard of people getting a brick through their window for interfering. If you tell the children not to write on the walls or not to play in the close or chop at the walls maybe somebody will spit on your door.

I feel that some of the tenants coming in are not as good as the ones that are going out. I feel that the Corporation is just sending in the dregs that's left in the city. Some of them are older people living in the tenements who could have had a Corporation house earlier, but never really wanted one, and who are now having the houses demolished.

Mrs O'Malley: I think the reason they don't want to come here is the rent. Maybe they were paying £7 a month, and it's £15 a month here. And there are very old houses in the centre with rents of only £8 a quarter. Some of those tenants have never been taught how to handle their money. We have our share of problem families.

Mrs Jamieson: Take a look at wages. The ambulance man near me has wages of less than £16 a week, after stoppages, and he has a family of six. His wife has to work at school cleaning. Otherwise he just couldn't manage. He's actually better off on social security.

He used to be a taxi driver, but he didn't like the work. He likes to be an ambulance driver, but he doesn't like the wages. A lot of people round here don't know about the Family Income Supplement.

Mrs McColl: I wouldn't mind moving further out, say to Cumbernauld, but they're closing one of the railway stations there. If you haven't got a car you're in difficulties in Cumbernauld.

Father O'Reilly: They are having a lot of trouble out at Cumbernauld because of redundancies at one big firm. They are too dependent on one big employer. The original idea of the new towns like Cumbernauld was not that the people there should be commuters, but that there should be industry out there. That would compensate for the higher rent. But if you're still working in Glasgow then you are taking on too much.

Mrs McColl: There's a lot to be desired in the shops on this estate, the vegetables, for example. They treat you on a 'take it or leave it' basis. You get fresher food in town than you do in the local shops. There's a difference in price too. You can go into the supermarkets in town, where you do save. We've only six shops here.

Father O'Reilly: When they build a new estate they should make provision for entertainment amd opportunities to create a community. With the exception of the shops the only facilities here are the three churches and the school clubs. It's the over-twelves who aren't catered for, probably because there aren't the people capable of dealing with them properly. It requires efficient leaders.

Mrs O'Malley: Some people are spending more on their homes, buying furniture and spending more time there, watching television.

Mrs Roberts: Personally, I'm not, because I haven't got any money to spend. My husband is a marine engineer, a skilled man. He gets good money. But he's been out of work for the last ten weeks.

Father O'Reilly: The modern housing schemes are laid out with pedestrian precincts, and the access for vehicles is such as to give the maximum amount of privacy and security. But the 'Old Guard' ought to consult the tenants as to what they want.

Mrs McColl: Does everybody here this afternoon agree that these three-storey buildings are better than multi-storey blocks?

Everybody: Yes.

Mrs McColl: The tenants' association have a sub-committee working as a face-lift committee. It helps to clean up the gardens, put up fences. We try to get all the people in one block to work together to improve their garden. We've had some successes in that direction. Then we got some derelict old garages pulled down which were always being set on fire by the children. We are building a children's playground by voluntary labour. We've made a start.

. . . in Liverpool

13. Growing up wild

MOLLY FLANAGAN · ADA BROWNE · MARION PETRIE
NANCY CUNLIFFE

MOLLY FLANAGAN: *Bickering over the baby*

Molly is beautiful in a typically Irish way, with long dark hair, blue eyes, and a lovely complexion. She wears a jersey, trousers, and smart black boots. Her husband, Michael, aged twenty-five, is four years her senior. He has a neatly trimmed beard. They live with their two babies and Molly's seventy year old father in a three-bedroom walk-up council flat in the centre of Liverpool. All the furniture is modern and new, except the old chair in which the father sits. The stereo record-player is a good one. There are plenty of children's toys around, and a small mongrel dog.

I got married at eighteen. I was working in a lab and Michael was a skilled man in the building industry – a joiner. We planned to save on our combined wages and buy a small house. We took out a £200 insurance policy. Then, after a few months of marriage, I started a baby.

We had saved the deposit for the mortgage, but my husband was not earning enough on his wage alone. You had to have £32 a week to get a mortgage on a suitable house, and he was only earning £24, so they wouldn't consider us. We've still kept up the life insurance policy, which, after two years, can be changed to a mortgage. But your wages have to be above the minimum required by the building society. We've given up the idea of a mortgage. They are all over you till you say you're a building worker. Building trade work is classed as casual work, even if you are a skilled man. That is because they get laid off in the winter when the frost starts. They may work for five or six months regular. But when you get frost it first of all affects the bricklayers. Then it works backwards and eventually the joiners are stopped too.

Today we've two children. One is two years and the little boy is three months. First we lived here with my parents. Then we went to live on the outskirts at Kirkby, about ten miles away. And now we've come back to my father's flat. I'll tell you why we left and why we came back again.

When we first got married we lived in this flat. My mother and I had always got on well between ourselves, till I got married. Then we had continuous rows. They nearly all started over the baby. We only had one before mother died. Michael and I believe in letting children cry if they aren't ill or overtired. But mother used to pick her up and spoil her and give her sweets. And Dad supported her in this.

This was the main cause of our bickering. It wasn't nearly so bad till the baby came. Once baby came on the scene there was trouble. You can't keep a baby outside all day.

Michael: In a way you are second man in the house. It's not your own house. You're second to the captain, you're second in command. If you use your authority with the kids, for example, your father objects. My mates at work tell me they are all in the same predicament.

It's like this with all grandparents. They're always giving them sweets and spoiling them. It's nice for the grandparents. They have all the pleasure of the children without the worry and responsibility.

Molly: Dad doesn't believe in shouting at a child. If Michael shouts at them I back him up. Then Dad says it's a united front against the children. And I'm stuck in the middle, between the two of them.

We were sleeping in the next bedroom to my parents and there are very thin walls. But this didn't worry us because my father is deaf and my mother was deaf in one ear and used to sleep with the good ear to the pillow.

So, because of the bickering we moved out to Kirkby. The rent was £4.06 a week including rates, compared with £2.38 a week here. Michael ran into trouble. He worked in Seaforth, which isn't too far from Kirkby. But there he had his joiner's tools, worth £100, stolen. His toolbox was locked up in the building. The firm weren't insured for theft – they had been broken into so often nobody would insure them. So he left the building trade. He got work as a driver for a firm and this week has been transferred on to office work for this firm. In a way it's promotion and the hours will be more regular.

We'd been in Kirkby three months when my mother died, leaving Dad on his own. He's over seventy and won't care for himself or bother to make meals or anything. I would have preferred that he came to join us out there rather than for us to come back here. But he wouldn't go because of his old mates.

We've altered a lot to suit Dad, and it's not fair on Michael. We got rid of every old piece of furniture in the flat except that chair there. That's Dad's. The only thing Dad pays is the rent and part of the groceries. We've altered mealtimes to suit Dad. Michael's got a small van to get to work in. He likes to work on it till it's repaired. But my Dad likes to go for a pint on Sundays at mid-day and then come home for dinner at three o'clock. So Michael, who attends to his van at his mother's, where there is an open space for him to park it well off the street, has to stop work to get back here for three o'clock.

There's the same difficulty here as in Kirkby. The children vandalise everything. They have their own gardens out there. At first the new residents took a great interest in them. Then they were wrecked by teenagers and fences were pulled down. So they felt it was not worth the effort of keeping up the gardens. Today there are only two gardens being looked after in six blocks. These two gardens are very near to the door, so that the tenants can keep a close eye on them.

There is a communal ground near here, but you can't let the children play on it because of broken bottles and rubbish. Everyone lets their children shout and get into trouble. That's why we would like to move away, so that our children don't get into trouble like them.

Mind you, there is a more friendly atmosphere here than on the new estate. They tended to keep themselves to themselves out there. Everybody was new. You didn't know the people upstairs or next door.

It was much more convenient in the new homes out there. For instance, you have an immersion heater. That was much more convenient than here, where you have to poke the fire up to get hot water. And it was much easier to clean. The houses are far more modern. They have a far bigger kitchen, with a larder and broom cupboard and a fitted wardrobe.

There's a lot of noise in these flats. They have four children upstairs. Our children are noisy. So you can imagine what it's like with four of them – and right over your head.

This place is due to come down to build a motorway. When your home is demolished I believe you can be more choosy about what sort of council house you go into. We'd choose to go to Fazakerley or Norris Green. They are not too far away from my father, who's elderly and has his friends round here in the centre of the city. Norris Green is very popular. If you like it's the crossroads of the city, convenient for buses and work.

We'd like to buy a house – a council house or a private house. At present Michael is earning a bit short of what is required for the kind of house we'd like. We are told that to get new houses at Maghull you don't have to pay a big deposit. You need roughly £1,400 a year minimum in wages.

It's very hard to save. We don't go out hardly at all. Last year we went out only at April and at Christmas. I knit a lot. But money goes on things like baby foods and baby soap. The babies' food nearly equals our grocery bill. It's about half on tea, butter, sugar, eggs and groceries like that, and about half on baby foods. Dad goes one-third on the groceries.

Michael is still paying for the van. He's trying to convert it into a caravanette, as we can't afford a holiday otherwise. We removed ourselves by van, and it's cheaper to use the van than buses. He'd have to use two buses to get to work and have to leave at 6.45 in the morning to get there for eight. It costs us £1 just to get the family to my mother's and back.

Very few couples can afford to buy their own homes. But I suppose you have to put up with it, the way it's always been.

ADA BROWNE: *A rough area*

Ada lives on her own on the top floor of a forty year old council walk-up tenement in the Exchange division of Liverpool. It is one of the early and less satisfactory council flats.

She is thin, bespectacled, worried looking. On the wall is a picture of Christ with an exposed bleeding heart.

I've been here six years. I lost my husband. Then I lost my married daughter and my little grandchild within a month of one another nine months ago.

I've got seven other children. They're all married. One of my sons comes a long way out of his way to see me on his way to night work. I want to go back to the old Scotland Road area I came from. I know more people there, and they are more friendly. They are not as rough as they are round here.

When they started clearing the old area I was the last to leave. They were going to put us into these flats. I didn't want one. I kept waiting because I particularly didn't want one with central heating. I wanted a firegrate and a coal fire. I was promised a ground floor flat, but I didn't get one.

My rent is £2 16s a week. It used to be £1 15s in Scotland Road. My rent is covered by a supplementary allowance.

I want a place with my own front door. It's rough round here in these flats. A woman can't stand on her own at the entrance on the street.

I've been taking sleeping tablets since I came here. Usually they put me to sleep. But I took one last night and it didn't work.

A few months ago I was wakened at three o'clock in the morning. I heard a rattle at the door. I got dressed and, without opening the latch, I looked through the door and saw a big man there, a very big man.

I was so frightened I knocked on the ceiling to the floor above with a brush. There was no reply. So I screamed for help. I was so upset I was sick all over the carpet. I decided to climb out of the window. Outside there were a lot of coffins in the churchyard. The church is being demolished to make way for the motorway and workmen had started to move the coffins out. I had to go past these coffins in the dark. It was terrible.

I ran on, not really knowing where I was going. Then I saw a police car. I said, 'Thank God. My prayer has been answered.' But it drove right past without seeing me.

Afterwards I saw a couple coming from a very late party. I told them, 'I want Springfield.' The man was so full of wine he didn't know where he was. In the end they got me home. We went up the stairs to my flat and there was this huge man sleeping in the passage outside my door. I don't know who he was. I think he had been drunk. The police came and took him to some hostel.

I want to move. My councillor says that he hopes to get the Council to make me an offer which will solve the problem.

MARION PETRIE: *Nowhere for the children*

Mrs Marion Petrie lives on the third floor of a four-storey block of old council tenements in Liverpool's Central ward. Her living-room is called the kitchen and the scullery is known as the back kitchen. They are separated by a curtain.

I want to move out of this place to a house, though I'm told this is impossible, unless you move away to the new towns, Runcorn and Skelmersdale. I want a house because I'd like to have a garden and my own front and back doors. I'd like rooms with a lot more space. Then my children could bring their friends home. I've got a girl of seventeen, a boy of nineteen and another girl of twenty-one. My oldest daughter, who's twenty-three, is married. My husband is dead.

We've been here twenty years. We have to eat in the back kitchen. There's hardly room for a table. The Corporation say you don't *have* to eat there. But we do so in order to keep the sitting-room free in case anybody comes to see us.

You take a place like this when the children are babies. Then, in no time, they've grown up. May won't bring her friends home. One of her friends came from Spain. May had been to work there for two years. When he saw the square where we live he said it looked like the bull ring. I call this block Sing Sing.

The rent is £2.38. I could afford to pay more, now that the children are older and I'm working myself. I wouldn't mind buying a house. But I'm forty-seven, and that's too old to start buying property. That's what I should have done in the first place. With a Corporation house you go on paying rent for the rest of your life.

It was worse before I came here. I was living in a room eight-foot by six-foot. I had no room between the bed and the cot. I brought my mother and father to live here. It helped them and I thought it would provide us with more points for a new house. They're both dead now.

I wouldn't mind going to the outskirts but I don't want to go to overspill. There's no chance unless you go there. My daughter says that if we did go to a new town the rents are much higher and there's not enough jobs there.

I asked a councillor why Liverpool no longer sold council houses. He said it was because they haven't got enough. There were too many in desperate need on the housing list, he said. Only when the people's needs were satisfied would they sell. At one time Liverpool built houses specially for sale. They only managed to sell two of them. He didn't think private builders were too keen on the council building for sale, because they'd prefer to make a profit for themselves.

NANCY CUNLIFFE: *The teacher who lives in a slum*

Nancy Cunliffe is dark and good looking. Although she left school at sixteen she has a BA Honours degree today. She took this the hard way, going first to a commercial school and taking advanced levels at night school, then to a training college. Next she taught in her own area for four years and studied at night for an external London degree.

This area is the kind of address you hid when I was a child. I eventually went to an intermediate school up the road. Anyone from this area was immediately relegated to the bottom of the class. My sister has recently been applying for jobs and will not put this address on her applications. She's a secretary, and she is now an assistant sales manager. They really hold the district against you. Managers have told her that when they get a letter from this district it's put to one side. Its reputation is very well known. My mother and dad will be able to tell you about it.

I had to go away to do a degree in the evenings because I couldn't get any extra money from the Council to continue education after I'd done a teacher's training course. So I had to do a part-time degree in London while I was teaching during the day.

There aren't any other teachers I've heard of who come from this part.

The houses don't look too bad from the outside, and some people say it's not too bad when they come inside. It's the way the people in the houses behave, and the gangs.

Her father: Unemployment is one of the reasons for that. Seven out of ten in this street.

Nancy: Poor education is another.

Her father: There isn't one shop in this street what hasn't been robbed, broken into. The insurance companies, which insure their windows and shops, won't insure them any longer, because of the vandals. The houses were built between the wars. The neighbourhood began to go down about ten years after the last war. The houses themselves aren't in bad nick. It's the people what's in them.

Nancy: But the amenities in them are very poor. Children are given no opportunity to lead any sort of existence except the one which happens here in the main room, where people are talking, watching television and having meals. They don't have a plug in their bedrooms which they could put in a record-player.

I've just got nowhere to go if I want to write or read or do anything privately. Mainly because of bad electrical fittings. These kind of things, we suppose, are going to be improved by modernisation.

We have a sitting-room, which everyone round here knows as the kitchen, plus what is really a scullery. You can't sit in it. It's known as a back kitchen. Then there's a bathroom with no handwash basin. Trying to keep any standard of hygiene in this place is difficult in the summer because unless you keep that fire roaring you can't have hot water and therefore can't have a bath, unless you boil buckets of water on the stove. You can't put an electric water heater in because of the wiring. We went into all that sort of thing. You can't have a washing machine because of the power.

Her father: If you happened to be using these things, all at once, such as the television and the iron and the light, everything would go bang. We can't even put a double adaptor on the plug, because the lights would fuse – not just our house but the whole of the block. We've been many hours in darkness. And once these go,

6

you're buggered. You can't get no alternative lighting. Unless you get candles. The last time there was a black-out we could not even get candles. What were on sale they were charging exorbitant prices for. Two bob for a candle!

In the morning there are three people getting up at the same time, all trying to cook the breakfast and wash themselves in that little scullery. There's nowhere else for them to wash.

Nancy: What would my ideal be? I won't go into ideals, I'll just go into what is possible for people like us to get, and what I know is being built at the time. They've got a very good scheme on an estate only about ten minutes' walk up the road. I don't know who the architects are, but they've definitely got the right ideas about how to rehouse people in the central area. First of all they have variety. There are lots of the terraced type of houses. They call them town houses now, two-storey houses. Then there are lots of maisonettes. It has been very interestingly planned. Not rows and rows. They all have different colours and different design.

We've applied but we probably won't get one, because this isn't a demolition area where we live. These houses are to be modernised. But we still want to move, because of the mode of living. It's soul-destroying. I know because of the housing shortage you have to cram people into multi-storey flats and blocks of flats of this sort. But they are putting the wrong sort of people into them.

I think it takes a very socially developed person to live in a community. This is probably opposed to all socialist ideals, but it's true. I've seen it. But I've also seen beautiful blocks of flats where everything has worked out fine, because the right sort of people are living there, people who have regard for other people's property. But these people here need a place of their own with a bit of a garden. They don't want adventure playgrounds. They want adventure in their own back garden. They don't have this. So they will go and vandalise any communal property. They are not given any reasonable conditions to live a private life.

When our family moved in here forty years ago my mother asked for a three-bedroom house. But she never got an exchange. The bedroom I shared with my sister is like a little boxroom. It's over an archway. Gangs congregate under it at night. I can't work at all in the evenings because of the noise. In fact I work here on this couch when everything is going on around me. And I'm marking sets of schoolbooks at least three or four nights a week – or at least trying to, with all this going on. It's becoming impossible. We're not snobs about living in the area. As far as I'm concerned I don't care. But it's becoming impossible now for me to do my job properly.

There's just simple things, like I'd like a little car. I teach in a comprehensive school, where there are two schools, and I should commute between the two. But I couldn't leave a car outside here overnight, because it would be wrecked by the kids, even if they didn't get in the car and drive off in it. They have methods of doing this.

When my sister and I who had been living away came home my mother applied for an exchange. They offered her a flat on the ninth floor of a multi-storey block. The vandals had broken the lift. She told them that her husband, a man of seventy-two, couldn't be climbing to the ninth storey. Though the houses were beautiful inside, so she was told, they have every convenience. But it's impossible for some of the people like there are round here to live in that way. When they have places they can call their own they do look after them and the children grow up with some sense of belonging. But they feel they are in some kind of remand home when they are in these blocks.

Her father: I think it's all a matter of education. They should get these vandals together and show them that the damage they are doing has to be paid for by themselves and their parents.

Nancy: But, Dad, education is a slow process and when you are expecting that of people round here you are expecting too much. It's got to develop slowly. And the only way to develop a sense of property is to give them a property of their own, with a front door, and a little bit of concrete round that door they can call their own.

Her father: The rents are going up here as far as they tell us. I think they'll have to get this Government out, first of all. If you get a good Labour Government in you can adjust these things, as far as rents are concerned. You can nationalise the land, for one thing. At the present time these big financiers, like Clore, they are making thousands of pounds without lifting their fingers. Charlie Clore found he'd made himself richer after half an hour by £895,000 when he took over some big stores. Not bad for half an hour's work.

14. Finding something better

DENIS TYLDESLEY · DAVID LONGBURN · JOE BECKETT

Sunday in a working man's club on a Liverpool housing estate. The three interviews are being held in a small committee room. From the adjoining hall come the emphatic voices of speakers attending a mass meeting of workers from a neighbouring factory. In the bar-room the round tables are completely covered with pint glasses of beer. Games of darts, cards and dominoes are in full swing.

DENIS TYLDESLEY: *A change for the better*

Denis is grey-haired, bespectacled, and developing a double chin. He is in his fifties and works as a storekeeper in a well known chemicals factory.

Years ago I had been living with an uncle and aunt. The uncle was found to have tuberculosis. When I was examined it was found that I had tuberculosis too. I was about thirty-five at the time. I spent just over a year in hospital and another eight months convalescent before I could return to work. I had been working in pharmaceuticals and this type of work was unsuitable for me. I had to change my job, though I could stay with the same company.

The local councillors were aware I had come out of hospital and took an interest in my case. They felt I should be rehoused. There was adequate provision at my mother-in-law's house, but they felt I ought to have a place of my own with two bedrooms, in case I had a relapse. There was just the wife and myself at the time.

We were given a ground floor flat with two bedrooms. Unfortunately there was a large number of large families in Liverpool who needed accommodation. I think that, very indiscriminatingly, they loaded these flats with very large families. As a consequence it was very very noisy. Hordes of young children were running upstairs to the flats above. If it rained they wanted to come into the hall. It was bedlam. Some of the mothers left the places dirty and put an awful weight on the tenants downstairs to keep the hall clean.

Of course we don't object to children. But you must provide enough space for them to spread out and enjoy themselves without infringing on everybody's rights and comforts. We've never been able to convince the Corporation that they should build a children's playground, despite the fact that they have densely populated the area by building flats.

When my youngster was about three and we were still living in that flat she obviously wanted to go out and play. So I decided to go out with her and that I'd take her to some school playing-fields which were only a matter of two minutes from the flat, walking along the road. I used to go on there and I became like the Pied Piper. All the children in the road used to follow me, because I suppose they felt that if authority came along I could deal with it. This went on for quite a long time. We went along regularly every evening in the summer and all the children would follow me. We used to use the various sandpits for long jump and so on. We had a great time. There was a keeper in a peaked cap who kept eyeing me. After a time he said, 'I've never really objected to your coming on here. When the children are with an adult you tend to keep them together and they enjoy themselves. But now you are getting too many, so I'm afraid I'll have to ask you not to come any more.'

I didn't want to involve the man in too much trouble, so we took the logical step. We started pressing through the Labour Party here to get something done about a playground. But every time we asked for land it was always scheduled for something. We still haven't got one. I think this is a tragedy.

All the noise and trouble began to affect my wife's health. She is a nervous type and started to develop from hay fever to a kind of asthma. So, though the flat wasn't too bad for me, it was affecting my wife's health. She gradually began to deteriorate. She was regularly going to bed with this complaint. The doctor understood the position, because his surgery was in the area. He made representations to the Medical Officer of Health, on our behalf, for a flat with a little less noise. It took some time. We had various inspections. This, of course, was the problem. There was nothing to complain about in the flat. It was ideal. It was very well built. It was the large number of children causing noise for the people living in the flats down below. Eventually the Corporation agreed I could have a 'like-for-a-like'. In other words I could move to another flat. After two to three years, during which time my wife's health had become pretty rocky, they eventually decided I could move to a new nine-storey, centrally-heated block.

The change was dramatic. My wife's health improved enormously. If we had had to stay in the previous flat I think things would have just got worse. I felt an enormous sense of relief. I could feel myself expanding. In fact I did better in my job. I think this was because I felt happier and knew my family was well situated. I only had to move a hundred yards to make all this difference.

DAVID LONGBURN: *Buying from the Corporation*

David, forty-one, is employed as a television engineer. He has a wife and three children, the oldest of whom is nineteen. He is wearing a smart blue mackintosh and has dark sideburns and wavy hair.

We used to live in a house over a shop. The conditions were very bad. We were there nine years and tried several times through the Council to be rehoused. They sent public health inspectors down. The inspectors who came were only bits of lads, trainees of about nineteen or twenty. They hadn't got enough experience to commit themselves to writing a report out on the extent of the damage.

The house next door had been completely bombed in the war. From the ground floor to the roof in our house there was a crack half an inch wide. If you put a match there it would blow out, even on a summer's day, thanks to the draught. The house was wringing wet all the time. The roof leaked too.

So I pursued the idea of buying a house in Bootle. I went all the way through. Then I found I was £30 short. I'd got my deposit, but I needed legal fees and all that. I didn't feel I was in a position to go into a house owing money and having no money left. So we decided to renege on this house and try and get a bit more money behind us. The solicitor was very decent. He agreed to forego all the legal fees. He had done all the searching.

The wife was getting a bit fed up with all the conditions. You would put wallpaper up and next week it was falling off. We were decorating two or three times a year – just to cover the damp. Then we had another youngster, and it became a bit harder to save. I kept going down to the councillors, and they told us there was nothing they could do as we hadn't got enough points.

There were four women working in the shop below, and the five in our family had to share the toilet. We had to clean it up too. Then because of a broken pipe the Corporation shut the water off, just after our baby had been born. So arrangements were made to wash the baby in the clinic, and for the public toilet to be kept open across the road for our benefit.

Then one week it teemed down. A friend got Councillor Dalton to come down at that time and see it. He was aghast. We had one of those galvanised baths and other receptacles to catch the rain coming through the roof. I had to twist the lights off, and fill all the lights in the loft with wax and pitch in case of explosion or fire. Councillor Dalton got the Chief Public Health Inspector to come down. The owner of the shop wasn't in a position to do the repairs. Eventually a closing order was put on.

It took about six months to get a house. When the news came the wife was overjoyed, really excited. The best I've ever seen her. So we moved into the house where we are now. It had been refused by other people because it wasn't up to their standard – a 1929 semi. But it didn't worry us, because we had about £110 we had saved towards a deposit, and we decided to put this into the Corporation house on Norris Green estate about five miles out. We bought a new fireplace and things like that, new gas fires. I bought new plugs and put them in the bedrooms. I had new window frames put in. Now we are buying it off the Corporation on a mortgage, which we pay monthly.

At first the mortgage repayments were higher than the rent. Now, three years later, our repayments are comparable with the rent. Next year the rents will be higher than our mortgage. I think we've done the right thing. The Corporation weren't even doing repairs. Since I've bought it I've put central heating in. It really looks a nice place now.

I've always done what I think is best for the family. The job that

I'm in has pretty good pay. If you use your cash right you can save up for the things you want. I put my priorities for the house and the children before anything else. Maybe other people want to back horses and go to the pubs every night. We haven't put ourselves in excessive HP. We don't live from week to week now. These last two years we've been able to go away on a nice holiday. Last year we went camping on Anglesey. At the present moment we are saving up to go to the Isle of Man and camp over there. It's something the whole family look forward to. Whereas if I came home and just gave the children a shilling and went out and had a few pints I don't think that would satisfy the kiddies for long. I think we all enjoy family life.

The wife works part-time. Both wages are put together and are paid into the bank. Our commitments are paid out of that. She's free to go to the bank and draw out for clothes or anything. We work everything down the middle. Mutual all round.

JOE BECKETT: *'Higher rents are making me buy.'*

Joe is thirty-six. He is sandy-haired, and wears an open-necked shirt and no tie. In his lapel is the badge of the Amalgamated Union of Engineering Workers.

Twelve years ago we were living in a slum area – Liverpool 3. You can imagine, with no facilities for hot water, what it was like with the young children. Then we came under the slum clearance order and we moved out. We were very fortunate insomuch as we came to a house with a garden front and back. The new rent in this council house was 29s 9d. We had only been paying a water rate of 4s 6d in the slum house, but it was worth the difference. Now the rent has become excessive, it's £4 8s for the same council house.

It's a parlour-type house. We can be critical of it now, because we are growing older and we expect more out of property. We are outgrowing the house, so to speak. We can only be thankful for the improvement in the house, but then we can be critical in the light of the changing situation and expect better things, and realise some of the drawbacks in the house. There's the lack of plugs in the house and restricted room in the kitchen for the wife. It's only about nine-foot by seven-foot. We've got a fridge, and we've had to take the door off the janitor's cupboard to put it in. As I say, people's housing expectations are rising.

There's a fault in this house which we didn't worry about in the beginning, because the contrast was so good. But now we notice that when you open the front door you have to walk right through to get into the back garden. There is no other access into the back garden. So if you are doing anything with a wheelbarrow you may have to carry the muck right through the wife's kitchen. Only the two houses at each end of the row have access to the rear.

Because of this fair rents business that they are bringing out, I've decided to buy the house, though it's against my own principles about buying council houses. I've been forced into that by economic circumstances. The wife is satisfied where she is and won't move, whereas I'd like to have bought a house outside. We're paying £4·40 rent, and it will go up to an 'economic' rent. On my wages as a steel erector, when I'm working that is, I can envisage that I'll be asked to pay, £6, £8 or even £9 a week. Well, I'm not prepared to do that, not for the facilities that we have. So I have decided to cut my losses, and buy the house. The approximate price of the house next door but one was given as £2,750. They are asking me £3,120 for mine only three months later. There's nearly a £400 difference in three months.

I wouldn't have much trouble with a mortgage. I'll put down a large amount of cash and get a part mortgage. At the present moment I'm on £45 to £50 a week wages when there's work. We are fortunate with the wife working and the older kiddies working. So I hope to take out a £2,000 mortgage, which works out at about £18 a month repayment over fifteen years, and pay the rest of the price in cash. It would be a bargain. I pay enough income tax so I'd get tax relief on what I pay for the mortgage.

15. Problems and proposals

GEORGE DELANEY · GEOFFREY ATKINS *(Headmaster)*

GEORGE DELANEY: *No facilities*

George, thirty-four, is a plumber who has worked on the Carinthia *and other famous ships. He is smartly dressed, and his manner is easy and cheerful as he talks.*

I live on an estate built thirty-three years ago. It has no facilities whatsoever. No clinics. Only a sub-post office. No facilities for youngsters. No community centre. There's one public house, which is quite notorious. There are empty spaces which have just become dumping grounds. Areas like these are used like a clearing house. People from slum clearance areas are forced into them. Because the properties have been up a long time and the families have grown up there are a lot of properties with three or four bedrooms just occupied by one elderly woman or man. The house is too big for them, the rent is too high. Finally they give them a flat, so there will be a lot of these houses becoming vacant. They will be used as a clearing house for slum areas.

From a shopping point of view my wife was better off in the old slum area than here, for it was far cheaper to live. There was more competition amongst shopkeepers. In our own area today there is a monopoly. There is the one fruit and greengrocer's shop and they dictate the prices. If you don't like them it means spending four shillings on a bus to go to town.

The schools are completely overcrowded. They haven't allowed for the population increase on this estate. So, in my view, it's an environmental slum. There are a tremendous lot of repairs outstanding. The people are being treated by Corporation officials as second class citizens. The officials get the idea that they are giving people something for nothing when they ask for repairs to be done. If you ask for landscaping they think you are crackers. Yet in the private suburbs of the city you always see gardeners tending the shrubbery. They've practically stopped sweeping the streets on Corporation estates. Though I'm in favour of municipalised housing I think that if we'd been given a decent grant when we moved out of our old house I think we'd have bought a house in a place we wanted rather than one we are forced into.

Liverpool has a lot of estates. Some are acceptable – some are not. They offer to rehouse you immediately if you will go to some of these estates. Norris Green is popular. Huyton is not. It's too far out. At night you see queues of men at the bus stops going back to their old pubs in the centre. Back to the old darts teams. The wives are left alone. It leads to the breakdown of some marriages.

GEOFFREY ATKINS: *Changes and improvements: a headmaster's view*

Geoffrey Atkins is a grey-haired, handsome, powerful man. He wears a light blue polo jersey and an open-necked shirt, since he is on holiday. His office is not particularly impressive. The furniture consists of a small table and two wooden chairs, green metal filing cabinets and glass encased bookselves. The window looks on to an ashphalt playground and a car park.

There's been a tremendous change in the housing situation. Where we are sitting right now there were these mid-nineteenth-century courts, with communal toilets. They were pretty grim. I've seen almost the whole of the area cleared of pre-1939 dwellings.

It's dangerous to make sweeping generalisations about the effect of rehousing on children. But I can say, in the wider context, that the people who have been hardest hit in all this have been the elderly people. The communication with old people has been extremely poor: when they are told they are going to move, how they are told, and who tells them. They tell me they now have better liaison officers, but I know I used to see heartbroken old people who had just received a notice. Sometimes the terms of the first letter were rather ambiguous, and left people wondering what was going to happen and when. I don't know if this has improved a lot. I feel very strongly about this, because I know so many of these old people. I've worked here for many years. It's a closely knit community: church, school and housing. Nobody lives more than a few hundred yards from us. I know the people and I feel that bureaucracy seems to have broken down in its relations with old people. Old people, if they have lived here forty or fifty years, obviously don't want to go too far away. And if they do go far away they don't want to be away from relatives. Some of them move when they are seventy-five. I suspect that they don't live long after the change.

For younger people the proximity of their father's work is an important factor. There was a postman I knew who operated in this area. He was moved out to Skelmersdale, which is about fifteen miles away. His job was in Liverpool city centre. This chap was an extremely happy and integrated personality delivering mail. He was looking forward to this new house. After he had been there I literally saw a deterioration in his personality. In fact he told me that he was living during the week with his mother or mother-in-law somewhere in the city area and then going out to Skelmersdale at the week-end. The reason for this is that a postman's job involves getting up, or being ready for work at 5.30. How does one get in from Skelmersdale at that time? These factors are even more important than the bricks and mortar.

If children are moved away from selective schools – if that isn't a dirty word – that's another consideration. And how far mothers are going to be away from grandmothers, who make a terrific contribution in these areas. (I have views about the non-participation of fathers – but I won't go on about that.)

Then I think they'd rather have anything, however small, than a house or a block they are sharing. Some of the happiest families I have known were those living in those tiny terraced houses across the road, because all of us like our little patch of ground and our four walls.

The schools should be more than a place for children between nine and four. We have an unusual development here: a primary school with a youth wing built on it. I think it's only the second in the British Isles where the Department of Education and Science has sanctioned a youth wing built on a primary school. They are usually associated with secondary schools. In addition we have a new nursery attached here, and recently we have opened a play centre.

So we are open from 8.30 in the morning till 10.30 every night, catering from the three pluses right up to the eighteen-year-olds.

The youth club is valuable. If the children are living in multi-storey blocks and there are four or five children they can't play round the door all day and all night. The club is first class in providing somewhere for the young people to go. They are trying to make the things they do more purposeful. Supervision is important. The authority have agreed to the appointment of three part-time youth leaders. Voluntary supervision is not good enough. Voluntary workers make a wonderful contribution, but they sometime only do it nine nights out of ten. It's on the tenth night that things can go very quickly wrong.

I accept the premise that these schools must be used to the full, but only if the authorities ensure there is proper supervision. Cleaning is terribly important. We must look on this as an entirely new thing. There are serious problems when schools are used out of hours. There is nothing worse than for teachers to come in and find that work which has taken a long time to prepare during the day has been ripped off the wall and tape recorders and tapes disturbed. We need a new look and better supervision. Housing alone is not good enough.

People should have freedom to live where they want to live. The population of Liverpool has gone down by 120,000, mostly to overspill. I don't want people to be made to live in multi-storey blocks round here if they don't want to but, given reasonable housing conditions, say like those provided in these town houses, I'm sure that seventy or eighty per cent of the people who have been moved would have stayed here.

Vast areas of houses have been denuded in one fell swoop. I don't know if this is peculiar to Liverpool. But I believe the same thing has happened in Manchester. Liverpool has taken a terrific knocking. Remember, too, that the university has churned up vast areas of the central part of Liverpool, again like Manchester. If people are going to live here let them be Liverpudlians. Let the students go and live on the outside. The powers that be must know this. Yet some people are even talking about providing accommodation for polytechnic students in this area. It's the people of Liverpool and their personality which have really put Liverpool on the map – not commerce or industry. You have only got to look at their quick wit. So let's put Liverpool people first and let the students do the travelling.

16. New houses for old

ELSIE WALDRON · MURIEL WESTCOTT

ELSIE WALDRON: *For the price of twenty fags*

*Mrs Waldron lives in one of four streets of houses which are newer,
bigger and better than most of the others in the ward. The bricks are well
pointed, and they are good engineering bricks – not the rotten porous
material so common in many old industrial towns. The tenants have
painted the outside of their houses dark red so that the brickwork looks
shiny. In many homes the doors and window frames have been brightly
and recently decorated. Some of the old wooden doors have been
replaced with glass or flush hardboard doors in more modern style. These
houses have windowed attics on the second floor, which make large and
comfortable bedrooms.*

*Four years ago they had one serious defect: no bathrooms or inside
wc's. Then the local authority, along with the landlord's agent, agreed
that this was an ideal improvement area. Using the standard Government grant covering half the property owner's expenditure, they went
into action – with gratifying results. Almost without exception the
tenants are highly satisfied customers.*

It's very good. The bathroom has been a boon. I've no young
children, but I've footballer sons, so you can guess what it means
to us. When I wanted a bath I had to go to my married daughter's –
that was before they altered our house. And it's so convenient having the toilet inside, instead of having to go outside to the backyard
toilet, especially at night.

We always wanted a bathroom, but we had no wish to leave this
district just to get a house which had one. My husband says he
wouldn't move out even if he had all the money in the world. We
have lived here all our lives. Our relations live nearby. My husband doesn't have far to go to his work. The shopping centre is very
handy. And these houses will be standing for another thirty years.

The agent approached us and asked if we would like to have it done. We said definitely yes. One bedroom has been converted into a bathroom and toilet. We can spare the bedroom because we have a bedroom on the first floor and, in addition, another on the top floor. They have put dormer windows in some of the attics in this street. Would you like to see it? (*She goes upstairs, opens the bathroom door and proudly displays the shining modern bath, wash basin and toilet.*)

Mind you, we decorated it and tiled it ourselves. We spent quite a bit of money on that. There's a good airing cupboard over the hot water cistern. They have removed the old toilet from the yard; it was an eyesore. It's rather a pity they didn't separate the bath and the wc in the new bathroom. It is pretty big, and they could easily have put in a partition. Sometimes you have to wait, although you easily put up with that.

The building contractor employed three men. They went down the street and did the job, one house after the other. They took three or four days at each house. We didn't have to move out.

It costs us five shillings a week extra on the rent. It's well worth it.

MURIEL WESTCOTT: *A huge success*

Mrs Westcott is a businesslike type of woman. She is neat; her house is neat; her life is neat. She goes out to work in the office of the Gas Board. Her house, though old and part of a long terrace, is furnished well and decorated well. The walls of the living-room are papered with dark green wallpaper, which has the appearance of velvet.

Mrs Westcott has a much less pronounced Liverpool accent than her husband and son, but she comes from the back streets of the city and is no snob. Her house is always full of neighbours, whom she regales with cups of tea and tasty ham sandwiches.

I've lived here all my life. I'm forty-five, and I've come from a large family. We had no bathroom in my childhood. We all used the public baths, so I definitely feel the joy of having a bathroom now. Plus the fact that we have hot water, too, which we didn't have in the older days. We used to have to boil loads of kettles on the old hob.

I've been married twenty-one years and my son is eighteen. I think it's far more beneficial to these boys to have the type of environment they've got now. When this improvement is completed it will be absolutely excellent. The back entries are being widened. They will be far cleaner. This will give the refuse men much better access to the backs of the house to keep them clean. I go out to work, a full-time job, for the Gas Board. This is a bit difficult if you are coming home and find all the dirty pots and you are continually swilling them. It helps your leisure to have these improvements. I think they will make it a smokeless zone, which will also improve the area.

I was in a Corporation flat. It was a wonderful flat, but it's not the same as having your own house. That's why we came here. We've lived here for six years. This is not such an old house as the one where I was born, it's approximately eighty years old, and it's structurally perfect. No dampness. The Corporation mortgaged it for me, and they really went through it. We bought it on mortgage. We paid £1,850 for it. I think it was worth it; compared with what has been charged for some of the houses round here I think I've got a bargain. I did have three bedrooms until I had the improvements. Now I've got two, but I'm quite happy about that.

Before the improvements we had to get washed in the kitchen sink, which I don't think is very hygienic, anyway. Certainly it caused a lot of problems. If you had visitors, no one could go through to the yard. There's two men in the house and I was the only female. I had to sort of keep guard on the kitchen at the time when I was getting washed.

There was a large piece in the *Liverpool Echo* from the Corporation telling us we could have 'New Homes for Old', sort of thing, and that people who were willing to go in for this grant, which at that time was a fifty per cent grant, could get help from the Labour Government. It was a Labour Government at the time. We thought this was an absolutely marvellous idea. So we wrote to the Corporation asking where we could apply for it, and eventually got down to the grants, which became even more later on, becoming seventy-five per cent grants. In my particular case the total cost was, I think, in the region of £450. I didn't get all this on the grant, because they don't allow windows, unless they are absolutely falling

apart. So I had to pay for all my own windows. Having the bedroom
made into a bathroom made it very inconvenient to have the old
type windows. My sink unit in the kitchen was in a very bad state.
I thought that if I was going to have all the other improvements I
might as well have the lot. So I had to pay for that kind of thing.
It didn't cover any of the plastering, except in the bathroom, where
I had some tiling done. The tiling I had to pay for. I also had a
shower and towel heating bar put in the bathroom. The house is
completely gas-heated, and the water too.

I pay off my half of the cost by a mortgage. This costs me £7 a
month over three years.

I had quite a long delay. It may have been on the part of the city,
because we were the first large area in the country to have this
improvements grant. Whether it was teething troubles or a slip up
by somebody I don't really know. I'm quite happy about it except
for a small plastering job, which I've got to have redone.

Having two washbowls makes a big improvement to the family.
We don't all have to wait for one another to get out of the kitchen
sink before we can get a wash in the morning before going to
work and going to school.

I think it's going to be an absolutely marvellous scheme in this
area, once it's completed. I think people *will* feel the benefit of it.
And I only hope that people will keep this up when it's done. There
are approximately 1,500 houses. Every house in the area has eventually to be improved on. I do believe that if the landlords are
refusing it at all, sooner or later the Corporation are going to take
over on a Compulsory Purchase Order and then the repairs will
be done. I agree with that, because there's no point in one person
having the area improved if somebody else is going to pull it down.
I think there is quite a large percentage of them which haven't got
baths at the present time. Those which have got baths are those
which have been put in individually by the people living there.

The smaller houses in the smaller streets, the small kitchen
houses – that's the old name for them – they just have four rooms:
a small living-room and a kitchen on the bottom, and two bedrooms
on the top. There's no room for a bathroom. There's far more
people having to live in those houses than there should be. In these
cases they're having their kitchenettes built onto the back, with a
bathroom on top of it, giving them two extra rooms. It's quite a big
job. As my small repairs cost a lot I hate to think what those

improvements cost. I think that eventually these landlords are going to get their money back anyway, the money that they are laying out for it, if the rents are going up to the extent that they are. Owner-occupiers could get it back in so many years if they repaid their mortgages at, say, two or three pounds a week.

But one tenant has told me that her rent is going up from £1.30 up to £3.65, which is quite a bit higher. They are not very happy about this, for the simple reason they know that this rent won't even be stopping at £3.65. When this housing Bill goes through it leaves them a wide open space to put the rents up again. A lot of these people are poor people who can't afford such a big increase. They might as well have gone down to the Corporation and gone into one of their brand new houses, where they would all be fitted out with their own bedrooms instead of being fitted into two bedrooms.

A lot of people who had the bathrooms put in themselves earlier feel a little bit of resentment, naturally, about this improvements grant, because they can't claim anything themselves. They have had to pay all their own cash out, before the scheme was introduced. I know one, in particular, who had hers put in only six months before this scheme came out. It was hard lines.

The majority of them who have had the improvements done with the grants are quite happy about the scheme. I am quite sure it makes some kind of beneficial change to the people. So many of them have never been used to having this luxury. It is a luxury when you have been used to going out of the area and into the cold streets, particularly wintertime, to go to the public baths and have a bath. They had to go some distance as there was none in this particular area.

There's an awful lot of little children round here. It must be marvellous for the mothers that have once had to bring the big tub in front of the fire to bath their kids, and now they can just walk upstairs and turn on a hot water tap, and throw the lot of them in. I don't think in this area that the lavatory being outside made such a difference. It was the hot water and the bath that was the main thing. I'd like to think that this particular area could be a huge success. Let people from other towns come and see it, and see exactly what can be done.

They're actually taking the traffic off this area eventually. They're making all one-way streets of it. They're planting trees at various points in the road to stop certain traffic. In the side roads the traffic will have to go slowly, so as to give far more freedom to the children to play. There's no area round here where the children can play at present. They've got to play in the streets. We are trying very hard for a community centre. When people get used to the idea of these trees it will probably make it look a lot nicer. They're going round asking all the people with dogs to keep them on leads and not let them free in the area. I do think people could check them a bit more than they do.

A local councillor commented: This is the first General Improvement Area in Liverpool, and there's another one to follow – a bigger one. Although they are supposed to have priority here it does seem that there is a hanging back by private landlords, who are not giving the co-operation that the owner-occupiers are certainly giving. It's to their advantage. But the tenants of rented property are losing out becuase of the waywardness of the landlords.

Liverpool Corporation have a problem on their hands. The number of improvements being done in this area is way below the figure they need to be up-to-date with their programme. When the Council changes political control in May we are going to have something done about this quickly. I think we should compulsorily acquire the property of landlords who are not co-operating. We've got to find ways of making these landlords toe the line, because these tenants are living in sub-standard conditions.

In Liverpool we have been told that in eight or nine years we are going to have a surplus of something like 14,000 Corporation dwellings. In other words, they're telling us that in eight years we'll have more houses than we know what to do with. I don't believe it. Because the whole programme is being based on a massive improvement programme, which is going to rely entirely on private landlords' co-operation, and I don't believe we are going to get it. The signs are already in this particular area, and I think it will snowball.

Also the Corporation are assuming that all the properties they own are good standard accommodation. As you know this is not true. Many of the Corporation properties these days should be classified as slums, because that's what they are. This supposed surplus they are talking about is being used as an excuse for cutting back on the Corporation building programme. If you talk to the officials concerned they will admit that the report on which this is based had a lot of ifs and buts attached to it. The controlling party is cutting out the ifs and buts and are cutting back on housebuilding in Liverpool, and are going to get rid of land to private builders which we think should be used for council building. Certain patches of land are now being sold off to private enterprise.

I think that in some cases the improvement of old houses is being used as an excuse for not building more new ones. This is the great danger. There may be an attempt to improve buildings which should be part of the clearance area, spending money on houses which are not worth improving.

These, in this part, are good standard houses, and there are many of this type throughout the city which could and should be given a long life. But because of the delay in this part, other areas which they planned to improve are deteriorating, so by the time they are reached they will be beyond improvement and only fit for slum clearance. There are 1,500 houses for improvement in this area and I guess a couple of thousand in the next for treatment. We intend also to have car parking areas and play spaces and traffic free areas.

Traffic is increasing all the time. It's infiltrating through residential areas, with the congestion on the roads these vehicles are finding a way through. It is being made difficult here so that only people living in the area will come into it. Anyone trying to take a short cut will find it will take them longer.

In another part we are going to have traffic free areas. But so many of these people have vehicles they have got to have access to their own premises, and also garage accommodation, which these houses don't have.

Part Two

What can be done about it

17. Why should rents be forced up?

All over the country tenants are beginning to realise the first effects of the Housing Finance Act. Far from being the 'Fair Deal for Housing', which is the way the Government describes it, this legislation is really a 'Raw Deal for Tenants'.

Its aim is to increase sharply the rents of 5½ million council tenants and their families by 1976, and to raise to 2½ times the present rates those of 1½ million private landlords' tenants who are still rent controlled.

This measure has nothing to do with providing better housing for those living in terrible conditions. It is a crude move to shift £200 millions a year from the Government on to the shoulders of the tenants. It is not merely a failure of the Government to keep down the cost of living: it is a deliberate increase in a major item in most family budgets.

This is how it will work.

Council rents

Council tenants will no longer have their rents fixed by their local authority. Instead, they will be decided by Government appointed bodies, the Rent Scrutiny Boards. Against their decision there will be no appeal. Councils may suggest a so-called fair rent. But the Rent Scrutiny Board figure will be final.

About one-third of the Boards are lawyers; another third are chartered surveyors or valuers. With some exceptions, the whole of their professional background biasses them in favour of high property values and, hence, of high rents.

There is already severe criticism of some of the supposed 'fair rents' fixed for private landlords' tenants, particularly in London. The Labour Party holds it is entirely wrong to fix council rents in a similar way. For when private rents are determined an amount is included to provide 'reasonable profit' for the landlord. Councils do not aim at making any profit at all out of their tenants. Why should they? What are now being introduced are not fair rents. They are profit rents.

Julian Amery, the Minister of Housing, and Peter Walker, the Secretary of State for the Environment, withheld information about what they thought the new rents would be despite frequent demands from Labour MPs. Then the cat was out of the bag.

They were able to get hold of a document circulating within the Ministry which stated the Government's estimates of what the unfair rents would be by 1976. They are printed in the accompanying table, along with the average rents paid in each region today.

	Average council rents 1970	*Average 'fair rents'* 1976 (*Ministry est.*)
London	£3.50 plus rates	£7.45 plus rates
South East	£3.13 ,, ,,	£6.49 ,, ,,
East Anglia	£2.16 ,, ,,	£5.72 ,, ,,
West Midlands	£2.43 ,, ,,	£5.72 ,, ,,
South West	£2.43 ,, ,,	£5.53 ,, ,,
East Midlands	£2.02 ,, ,,	£5.14 ,, ,,
North-West	£2.23 ,, ,,	£4.66 ,, ,,
Yorkshire & Humberside	£2.02 ,, ,,	£4.56 ,, ,,
North	£2.08 ,, ,,	£4.38 ,, ,,
Wales	£2.39 ,, ,,	£4.18 ,, ,,

If a local authority housing committee refuses to implement the scheme, the Government has given itself power to supplant it by appointing a Housing Commissioner in its place, and to withdraw all subsidies.*

*In May, 1972, the Government indicated a sudden uncertainty about its intentions. The Birmingham Corporation housing authority, then under Conservative control, wrote to Mr Amery estimating their 'fair rents' on quite different criteria from those specified in the Bill, and also at a far lower level than indicated in the above table. Mr Amery quoted the figures in the Chamber,

Housing subsidies

If the idea were to *redistribute* subsidies, giving some a little more help and others a little less, then it might be possible to argue a case for it. What is involved in this Bill, however, is a sweeping *reduction* – which is quite a different matter. They are to be slashed by up to £200 millions a year compared with what they would have been by 1976.

Private landlords' rents

These will be raised for 1.3 million tenants who still remain rent controlled. Their rents will not just be doubled: they will be increased on average to more than $2\frac{1}{2}$ times the present figure. We know this because this is the rate of increase which is revealed in the statistics MPs have been able to extract from the Department of the Environment concerning rents already decontrolled.

These will be, for the most part, the very worst houses, including homes lacking a bath, hot water and inside wc and slum houses not yet scheduled for demolition: houses so bad that the tenants often say, 'The landlords should pay us for living in them!'

Another evil feature of this vicious Act is that landlords and tenants are permitted to 'agree' a rent without going to the Rent Officer. An exorbitant rent will in many cases be extracted from the highest bidder for an empty flat or house and the landlord will get him to sign a document that he regards this as a fair rent. Though the tenant can go to the Rent Officer subsequently, he is unlikely to do so if he has signed such a letter.

The rent increases will not be applied in one fell blow – Ministers fear the reaction would be too dangerous for them if this happened. They will be staggered. But a big rent increase remains a big rent increase, even if it is staggered for council and private tenants.

---

thereby giving them some credence, but declined to say whether or not he approved them. At the end of May he had still not announced a decision.

This development may mean that – thanks to the strength of opposition to the Bill – the Government have decided to make a partial climb down and retreat to consensus politics, as it was forced to do in certain other fields. At the moment of writing (June 1, 1972) it is not possible to say whether this was a real retreat or merely a move to lull opponents of the Bill into dropping their campaign.

Even that is not the end. For every three years there is to be a 'review' of rents. This will certainly mean a further increase rather than a reduction.

For private tenants the increases are due to start in January, 1973. There seems to be no end to rent rises in sight.

Those rent rebates: Julian Amery's little trick

Many people who have read about the Government's plans – and most newspapers have played down the criticism – have been misled into thinking they are going to enjoy rent *reductions*!

Mr Amery has published little tables which show, for example, that if you are a married man earning £30 a week before stoppages and have a wife and two children, paying £5 a week rent you will receive a rebate of £1 weekly.

What is the trick? It is that the £5 plus rates will be the *new* rent fixed under this Act. Yet that tenant might be paying only £2 a week plus rates today. So his rent will go up from £2 to £5 and then come down £1 because of the rebate. So he will be paying £4 a week plus rates, or twice the rent paid at present.

A giant means test

Rebates will be considered only if tenants apply for them. The whole scheme is based on the assumption that everyone is prepared to put his hand out. It is a false assumption. There are large numbers of working people who are too proud to have the details of their family poverty examined by hordes of officials. Many workers find it exceedingly difficult to fill up complicated forms, for not everybody is a chartered accountant. Then, there are those who never learn about the possibilities.

Out of more than 200,000 Greater London Council tenants, only 18,000 receive a rebate. Only four out of ten of those the Government expected to apply for a Family Income Supplement have done so, despite wide and expensive advertising of the scheme.

In Birmingham there is in operation a scheme to give rent rebates to private landlords' tenants. There are 60,000 such tenants in the city. How many have applied for a rebate? One thousand. And of those, only 250 have received a rebate.

There will have to be a means test to discover what the family income is. The wife's income is included. Children over eighteen will have to be considered. If one of them is earning more than the father, the latter can be considered as the tenant, which is likely to lead to friction in many families, perhaps even to their break-up. Family incomes are continually altering, say, when the breadwinner is knocked off overtime or when the mother is going to have a baby and has to stop work. So there will have to be a *continuing* means test.

The Act says it must be carried out at least every six months. The local authorities will have to employ a mass of officials to carry out the investigations. Maybe this is the Government's solution to the unemployment problem. It will certainly not be a solution to the housing problem.

The Scrutiny Boards will appoint officials to visit and assess properties in their areas. If one of these Scrutiny Officers asks to come inside a house to examine it, a tenant can be fined £20 if he refuses him admission. (An Englishman's home is his castle!)

Increasing house purchase prices

Many tenants, faced with the threat of doubled rents, are beginning to say to themselves, 'Well, if I've got to pay such an exorbitant rent I might as well try to purchase a house, since at least I'd have something to show for the money – even if I can't really afford to buy.'

What will be the effect of this unnatural increase in the pressure to buy houses? Undoubtedly, it will be to raise even more rapidly the price of houses. If rentals of private homes go up, then so will their capital prices – and their prices on the market.

Most workers are dependent on council housing because – even with a mortgage – they cannot afford to buy their own houses. But since May 1968, when Conservative majorities took over nine out of ten Councils, there has been a drastic fall each year in the number of council houses started. This decline will now become even worse. For there will be great numbers of families living in terrible housing need who will be unable to go into a council house. Their rents, even after rebate, would be too high for them to pay.

Similarly, councillors will be discouraged from starting new housing projects by the knowledge that they will be forced to charge excessive rents for them – a highly unpopular and electorally damaging action. Whilst the originators of the Housing Finance Act are Ministers and top civil servants in Whitehall, the obloquy will fall on councillors in the Town Hall. For it is they who are compelled to send out the rent increase notices.

THE ALTERNATIVE

So long as Britain has a government of the present political complexion it will be difficult to get rid of the Housing Finance Act and its injustices. However, on the assumption that it is replaced by a Labour administration at the next general election, what would a fair, progressive and practicable policy involve?

Repeal of Housing Finance Act

There should be a repeal of the present Act. Resentment of it is so great and so widespread amongst tenants and working people that anything less than complete repeal would not satisfy their wishes. That does not mean that it does not include a few acceptable clauses. (It would be odd if, in an Act with 103 clauses and 160 pages, it did not.) It would be possible to reinstate the few good parts at the time of repeal. A similar situation applies to the Industrial Relations Act, against which the anger of trade unionists is so great that only outright repeal is agreeable to Labour's rank and file.

Restoration of subsidies

Restoration of the national subsidies to council housing is essential. For 1970 these totalled £157 millions a year from the Treasury and £65 millions from the local authorities. These subsidies are naturally growing annually as more council houses and flats are built each year. So it will be necessary for the next Labour Government to restore to housing the subsidies to the total which would have been payable annually at the time they take office, under the pre-1972 legislation.

Although most of our national newspapers think otherwise, there is nothing shocking or unique about subsidising housing. Nearly every country in the world does it. For example, in West Germany, where most new housing is for owner-occupation, those of relatively low incomes receive a generous subsidy from the regional governments in the form of interest-free loans, or loans at one per cent or some other nominal figure, on the first part of their mortgages.

Reactionary newspaper proprietors constantly strive to drive a wedge between owner-occupiers and tenants. In reality they both suffer from the same burden – that of high interest rates on building loans. The truth is that owner-occupiers receive a higher state subsidy than do council tenants. The former were granted £302 millions in tax relief on their mortgage payments during 1971, compared with the £222 millions for council tenants mentioned earlier, after adding help from the local authorities. The householder buying his house on mortgage receives an average hand-out from the Government of £60 a year, compared with £44 for the council tenant from combined national and local sources.

Further, the richer the house purchaser and the more lavish his house the greater is the subsidy he receives. A man paying income and surtax at the marginal rate who obtains a £30,000 mortgage on a mansion gets the little sum of £2,100 a year or £42 a week from government funds.

I am certainly not proposing that the next government should remove the tax relief on mortgage payments. What is, however, manifestly unfair, is to maintain that subsidy whilst slashing it for council tenants. Justice demands that the council subsidy be fully restored.

At the same time it is reasonable to suggest that a ceiling be placed on mortgage payments on which tax relief should be granted. It might be fixed, for example, at £6,000 in the provinces and £9,000 in London. Above that the rate of relief should be tapered off to nil on the balance of the mortgage above a certain sum.

Subsidies cost money – though it is a tiny sum in relation to total government spending. The Opposition should not dodge the issue. They should state now that to house people in sufficient numbers at rents they can afford is going to cost money, and they are prepared to spend it.

Abolish the 'fair rents' system

The 'fair rents' system of determining rent levels (the market value of the property, less a small deduction to allow hypothetically for the shortage factor) is unjust and unnecessary. What should the alternative basis be? The function of determining council rents should be returned to the local authorities. They must *not* be expected to produce a surplus or profit.

Up to 1972 most local authorities operated the pooled historic costs system. They charged tenants enough rent – and no more – to cover the original cost of the house and land, plus loan interest, repair and management charges. Because many council houses were built before 1960, when costs were relatively low, reasonable rents could be charged. Since then, with higher building, land and interest costs, the more recently built houses and, in particular, flats (which are generally far more expensive because of deep foundations, lifts, and the need for caretakers) would have brought about such dear historic rents that they would be above the means of ordinary workers, even with subsidy. So they have been spread over the whole pool of that particular authority's stock of council housing. This has meant increases in rent for tenants of the older properties, but it has greatly helped the newcomers and has allowed much needed new building to take place.

From pooled historic costs, estimated in this way, a reduction has been made by means of national and local subsidy. Every system of renting contains some anomalies. This, however, would seem the fairest. The main objection is that it penalises tenants in areas where the proportion of new housing to old housing is a high one, where there is only a small stock of old houses built at low cost over which to spread the higher charges. This especially applied to new towns, where there is virtually none of the earlier property. In these areas an additional special subsidy should be paid from the Treasury so that new buildings can proceed at reasonable rents.

Interest-free loans

Consider an average council flat costing £5,000, including land. By the time interest has been paid on it at the current rate of $8\frac{7}{8}$ per cent for the next sixty years (the usual borrowing period) it will cost the little sum of £26,788. Of this total no less than £21,788 is interest.

And who pays this colossal burden? Mainly the tenant. Out of every £1 paid in rent, sixteen shillings goes to pay, not for the building workers' labour or the materials, but for the interest charge. Admittedly the severity of the interest charges would be mitigated in the future to some extent if inflation should continue, since the real value of later interest instalments would diminish. However, there is no law that inflation must take place at all times. It has not, even in recent years, balanced the quintupling of the original cost. And – certainly in the early years of the loan repayment – it makes only the smallest recompense for the high interest costs.

Yet when the Government builds a motorway or a battleship it does not pay one penny in interest. It builds it out of revenue – for cash payment. If houses were paid for like that they would cost only one-fifth of the total price.

The cost of a year's total of council houses building is about £800 millions a year. It would be possible to finance the whole programme in this way. Even if that is a big sum it is less than one third of our annual arms expenditure.

A more modest suggestion would be that, to begin with, the Government should spend £200 millions a year in this manner on council housing. Then the enormous financial saving on this quarter of the houses constructed could be spread over the total programme.

This may be a new proposal, but it is not the worse for being so. When broached last year no convincing argument was raised against it. The Government found other ways of burying the scheme.

Share the burden more widely

Another reform would be to remove from local authorities' housing revenue accounts items which should properly be shouldered by the whole community rather than by council tenants alone. For example, it is of great benefit to a town as a whole that a slum should be cleared. This usually entails extremely expensive land and compensation costs, demolition charges and interest charges on the purchase price until it is used for rehousing purposes. These should be charges on the rates – not just added to council rents. Similarly, council tenants are often made financially responsible for expense involved in providing special housing for the elderly. Here, too, all ratepayers should contribute – which of course includes council tenants but should not involve them exclusive of others.

Extend the option mortgage scheme

The option mortgage scheme should be extended to help would-be house purchasers on low incomes. From April, 1968, they have been able to enjoy the same rate of relief on their mortgage interest as if they were in the full income tax paying bracket. Instead of paying, say, 8 per cent on their mortgages they pay only $5\frac{1}{2}$ per cent. But is $2\frac{1}{2}$ per cent subsidy enough? Should not low wages earners receive *more* help than those on higher incomes? Why not double the allowance to 5 per cent and make the subsidy really worth while?

An additional help to the little man buying his own house is to grant 100 per cent mortgages. Some local authorities already make such loans to ratepayers, provided the valuation of the property is up to the purchase price paid. Could not building societies also ask for a lower proportion of deposit than they do now? After all, 'There's nowt so safe as houses'. They have a truly adequate security.

Another aid to owner-occupiers would be to reduce conveyancing costs. Solicitors receive grossly inflated payment for what is, in most cases, a purely clerical job, often requiring little more than the writing of a couple of letters. Mr S. G. Carter and his National Home Owners' Association have shown that it is possible to break the lawyers' monopoly in this field and have the task done by laymen.

18. The way out of the mess

There are some politicians, professors, property owners and newspaper pundits who believe that the solution to the housing problem can be summed up in two words: higher rents. It cannot. The way ahead for the homeless, elementary as it may seem, is to build more houses, and at prices or rents they can afford.

The need is colossal. In this book I have taken just a few drops from the sea of human misery caused by the housing shortage. These individual cases are not horror stories. They are, unfortunately, typical of the experiences of several millions of families: eleven million men, women and children in houses without a bath, hot water or inside lavatory; the overcrowded; the young couple who have to live with their in-laws; the slum-dwellers; those with no roof at all, forced to sleep in hostels for the homeless. Government estimates are that there are roughly $1\frac{1}{2}$ million slum homes unfit for human habitation and requiring demolition, plus approximately $4\frac{1}{2}$ million dwellings lacking one or more of the basic amenities just mentioned, or needing substantial and pressing repairs. (At the average of three people to a dwelling this means that about 18 million people are affected.)

If we add to this total the numbers of dwellings needed to house the growing population, the extra number of separate households caused mainly by earlier marriage and the increasing number of people living on their own, to their seventies and beyond, the reason for a vast building programme becomes obvious. Many housing experts, such as Professor Colin Buchanan, Anthony Crosland and Shelter spokesmen, agree that without half a million new homes a year the housing problem will be with us for decades. This was the target accepted by Labour in its 1964 and 1966 election programmes.

I should like to see the Labour Party give a pledge that they will raise the building programme to half a million within four years of being elected to government. There will doubtless be those who think it foolish to publish a target figure on the grounds that, if the Government fails to reach it, there will be damaging political repercussions. I do not accept that argument. It would be far better to proclaim the 500,000 target – and adhere to it at all costs.

Admittedly no Government has ever yet reached that figure. For eight years up to the end of 1963 just under 300,000 houses were built each year by the Conservative administration. In the following year (which was a general election year) the number rose to 366,000. Thereafter it went up annually under Labour till it reached, in 1968 an all-time record of 413,000 in 1968. Then it went down in both sectors. In the private sector it was because the Government had been knocked off course by the pressure on the pound, devaluation, and the ensuing credit squeeze. In the public sector the constant fall in council house starts (see the accompanying graph) was due to a different reason. In May 1968, nine out of ten Town Halls in the country went Conservative. With some exceptions the new majority leaders were not enthusiastic about council housing. They disliked it for ideological reasons.

The Rt Hon Peter Walker, MP, himself now the Secretary of State for the Environment, speaking in Manchester in June, 1969 to a Conservative housing conference said:

> I hope that Conservative councils will take great care to resist the temptation to go on building council houses for all sorts of seemingly good purposes ... New Conservative housing chairmen have a great tendency to prove to the Socialists that they can build even more council houses than their predecessors, and all sorts of perfectly good social reasons are advanced for doing so. I do not mind their finding the good social reasons for doing so, providing that at the other end they find good economic reasons for releasing many other council houses for owner-occupation – houses for which there is no social argument for their retention in the public sector.
>
> The stock of 30 per cent of housing now in local authority hands is far too high with the level of wages in Britain. The average industrial wages is now more than £23 a week. With that level of wages we do not need one third of the stock of houses to be council houses. I hope that under the next Conservative Government there will be a shift in the other direction.

Whilst he later denied meaning this, I have the verbatim text of his speech, which is unmistakeable.

This cut-back in council house building has worsened under Mr

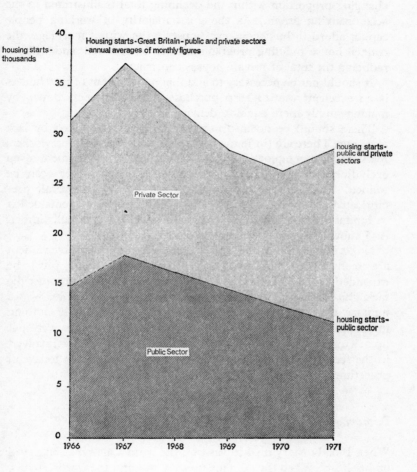

housing starts-
thousands

Housing starts-Great Britain-public and private sectors
-annual averages of monthly figures

40

35

30

25

Private Sector

20

15

10

Public Sector

5

0

1966   1967   1968   1969   1970   1971

housing starts-
public and private
sectors

housing starts-
public sector

Walker's Government, although there has been an increase in private house building which has nearly compensated for it. (The changing proportion within the declining total is illustrated in the accompanying graph.) As the great majority of working people cannot afford to buy their own houses, even with a mortgage, the council house building programme must be restored, and without reducing the total of private houses constructed.

It should not be necessary to add that a big output of new houses is an excellent way to keep purchase prices and rents down, by making supply more equal to demand.

There should be no insurmountable obstacle provided by lack of labour. There are (in January 1972) 147,000 construction workers registered as unemployed by the Department of Employment, even excluding Northern Ireland. Additional skilled workers can be trained. Their output can be supplemented by industrial, pre-fabricated factory building. There is no balance of payments deficit to hinder us from obtaining the main imported material, timber. As I show later, the additional money can be found.

No. It is chiefly a matter of will. If the public and the Government are really determined that the housing programme must be expanded, this will be brought about. The problem must be tackled as a national emergency, by a great, planned, effort – as a military campaign would be in time of war. There is nothing impracticable about this. In 1939 huge ordnance factories were put up in a matter of months, and nine million men and women involved in the forces and war factories. We need a similar drive today, in peacetime.

Improving old houses

When Bloody Mary died it was said the word Calais was engraved on her heart. When they dig me up they will find the words, 'baths, hot water and inside lavatories' inscribed on mine. It is the lack of these basic necessities of modern civilised life which is so bitterly felt by most of the ill-housed families interviewed in this book. In many towns one in five houses is without these amenities. In Glasgow alone there are 76,000 houses without a bath. That means roughly a quarter of a million men, women and children. There are 32,000 without an inside wc.

There are three million homes without a bath, hot water and inside wc. That accounts for nearly one family in five. In the year 1972, in the so-called affluent society and in the so-called welfare state, we can send satellites to the moon – but cannot put a bath in the house.

Many of these homes, of course, are officially condemned as unfit for human habitation. They must be pulled down and replaced as soon as is humanly possible. But what about the remainder? Even if we reach a target of half a million a year, numbers of these older houses will have to stand and remain inhabited for thirty years or more. Moreover, large numbers of them are structurally sound. It is the lack of the essentials – bath, hot water and wc – which makes them so undesirable to live in.

Many of the residents, given those three amenities, do not want to leave. Take the case of a railwayman, living near his depot, who starts work at three o'clock in the morning. How can he move to overspill, maybe ten miles away, and get to his railway station at that time in the morning?

The financial saving in improving, rather than demolishing, a house is obvious. In Salford, which has improved more than a thousand houses so far, the average cost of the combined bathroom and lavatory is about £220. In contrast a new council flat, including the land, may cost £5,000.

Generous grants have been provided by both governments for improving these older houses. Half the cost, up to a maximum of £400, must be provided on a standard grant, when requested; and a discretionary grant of up to half of a £2,000 improvement is also available for more extensive modernisation. As an additional incentive landlords are permitted to take their properties out of the existing rent control. This means an increase, on average, to 2·6 times the previous rent, plus extra rent to cover the improvement. (This was permitted by the Housing Improvement Act, 1969. It allowed the ending of control even where the house already possessed these amenities. Two other Labour MPs and I voted against our own government on these clauses.) A further incentive has been to raise the Government's contribution to 75 per cent of the cost in the development areas, mainly to encourage employment there.

Owner-occupiers and local authorities have, very sensibly, taken advantage of these offers in a big way. (In some areas there has been a veritable bonanza for modernising week-end country cottages.)

But, despite the enormous carrot, the majority of private landlords have not. They just won't be bothered. The best way to overcome this resistance is for the Council to set up general improvement areas, in which every house needing attention will receive it. So far 135 have been established. Where private landlords refuse to co-operate the council has the power to step in, do the job and then step out again. This seems to some of us likely merely to encourage these property owners to sit back and do nothing. The better alternative would be to authorise local authorities to acquire the houses compulsorily and carrying out the work themselves.

There are many new-found friends of improvement who wish to see it as a substitute for new building. The country needs *both*. A crash programme by the Government should be for 500,000 new homes *plus* 200,000 improvements annually.

Who owns the land?

'God gave the land to the people' was the cry of the reformers many years ago. Unfortunately they do not possess it at present. It is the property of a few landowners who can hold the community to ransom.

Not long ago there were some strange happenings in the Lea Valley in North London. Mr Ernest Pallett, a small farmer, owned nine acres in this area. The land was valued at about £500 an acre, a total of £4,500. Then one day the Ministry announced that there was to be some encroachment into the green belt, and that houses might be built in the Lea Valley. Overnight – and I mean literally overnight – his holding of £4,500 became worth £80,000. Within ten days, Mr Pallett received eight offers, each of more than £72,000.

One very frank MP, now retired, has related how he bought some land for £36,000. That was its value for agricultural purposes. Then permission was given to build houses. Such is the demand for building land that, irrespective of the owner's intentions or wishes, the value of that land suddenly soared to a million pounds.

In January 1972 it was reported that half an acre of land had been sold in Hampstead for housing purposes at a price of £215,000. One can only imagine the cost of the flats constructed there.

The price of land has risen so seriously that the Greater London

Council pays on average £1,600 for the land for a single flat – not a block of flats. That adds about thirty shillings a week to the rent for the land alone, before a single brick is laid.

A vital principle is at stake here. Suppose there is a plot of land, perhaps the size of Wembley stadium, somewhere on the outskirts of London or another big city, being used to grow potatoes. Then the authorities build a main road along one side of it and provide a bus service. Nearby a large factory is erected. Electricity, water, drainage, gas and telephone lines are supplied to the area. And the growth of population is such that people are driven to find new districts, including this one, to live in. Then – without any effort by the owner – once permission is given to use that land for building purposes the value of the territory automatically soars. In a single day that potato field turns into a goldmine.

The all-important principle is this: where land increases in value, not through the efforts of the owner, but through those of the community, then that increase should be returned to the community which created it.

It was to put this principle into practice that the Town and Country Planning Act was introduced in 1947. The aim was to take land into public ownership, once and for all, compensating the owners to the tune of £300 millions. When the 1951 election put the Conservative Government into office they started to dismantle this legislation. The last controls were removed in 1959. From that moment the sky was the limit. Fortunes were made by speculators out of the land racket, and the community suffered.

This was the background to the Land Commission Act, which was passed by the Labour Government in the summer of 1967. It laid down that, when land was sold, the full market price had to be paid. But the seller had to pay to the Government a levy equal to 40 per cent of the difference between the previous use value of the land, e.g. the £36,000 when used for growing potatoes, and the enhanced value once planning permission was given, e.g. the one million pounds in the case mentioned above. Owner-occupiers were exempted.

Writing at the time, I expressed the view that this could possibly be a great step forward, but that I had my doubts. First, for the obvious reason that if a different Government were elected the Act would be scrapped. (It transpired that the Land Commission Dissolution Act was one of the first measures introduced after

June 1970.) Secondly, I feared that the big property owners and their lawyers and surveyors would find ways to circumvent the legislation, which, to a considerable extent, they did.

Thirdly, a tax on increased values would not necessarily mean halting the rise in land selling prices. And fourthly, the landowners would go on strike and refuse to sell unless compulsory powers were used. In fact only a few hundred acres of land were bought by the Land Commission before it was dissolved.

The Act was given only three years to bite. Nevertheless there was one beneficial result: part of the increase in value was siphoned off to the community. In the first years it was only a relatively small sum, but up to £31 millions a year would have been yielded by 1973, above what would have been secured by capital gains tax, if the law had not been revoked.

Today, there is once again no control, and astronomical land prices are having to be paid. The greatest land boom of all time is now taking place. The inner boroughs of London wish to buy land in the outer boroughs – the only areas available. Even if the objection of the latter is overcome – as it must be – the price required will be prohibitive.

Therefore effective action is required. It will not be taken by the present Government, whose interests are traditionally linked with those of the landowning class. Evidence of this is provided by the speed, enthusiasm and unanimity with which it scrapped the Land Commission Act.

The Labour Party has set up a working party to consider proposals for dealing with the land problem. Amongst the rank and file there is a feeling that to reintroduce the Land Commission legislation would not be good enough. Indeed at the 1971 annual delegate conference (the Party's supreme policy-making body) a resolution was carried asking the national executive to draw up plans for public ownership of land.

I agree with this. The plans will have to be clear and relatively simple, so that the public will see how they will benefit and so as to avoid providing a lawyer's paradise. They should be available for implementation early in the life of the Government. And they should aim at making it difficult for a subsequent Government to unscramble them.

Wanted : better planning, design, building

Amongst those who have been rehoused there are many satisfied customers, and there are many who are anything but satisfied. Bitter disappointment is often felt by parents who have waited for a decade or more, longing for a better home, only to find the new accommodation has major disadvantages. For every example of good planning, design and building a bad example can be quoted. It is a remarkable thing that these serious errors have been made by men who have given years of devoted service to the community. There is no point in crying over spilt milk, but it is imperative to learn the lessons from unhappy experience and ensure that these mistakes will never be repeated.

It is essential that, when slum areas are demolished and old and closely knit communities rehoused, care is taken to see that neighbours are kept together. Where care *has* been taken, the newscomers usually express delight with their new homes – even in multi-storey flats, which few of them wanted.

Too big an area of a city centre should not be demolished at one fell swoop. In some cities this has happened, with a huge area left idle for several years, and with the former inhabitants exiled eight, ten or twelve miles to the perimeter of the conurbation. By smaller clearance schemes it is possible to provide new homes near at hand through a leap frog process. The worst conditions of all are being experienced by those left behind in clearance areas after demolition has commenced. Alternative accommodation of the required size and kind must be available for all residents before rehousing begins.

In future, huge expanses of land in city centres should go to rehousing local families rather than for university buildings. Why should not the universities be built on the outskirts, instead of people's houses being put up there? This is not written in any anti-student attitude. Most students would themselves admit the fairness of giving priority to families who have lived there for years.

Just as there is a need to give applicants a choice of where they are to be rehoused, so is it only right that they should be given some choice of the kind of accommodation. There are towns where people have been given no alternative to multi-storey flats. A minority like them; the majority do not. It is significant that Liverpool has recently decided on a policy which would exclude families with children under fourteen years of age from high-rise building; while Glasgow has decided to stop building any multi-storey blocks at all.

Where flats are built in the future much greater care is required than has been exercised in some areas. As one mother said to me: 'The architect who designed this flat ought to be forced to live in it for six months.' He would certainly become a better architect if he consulted the residents of the block. Better insulation against noise from neighbouring flats, particularly those on the floor above, is called for. More important is the need to provide playgrounds for children up to the age of about twelve. There should also be indoor playgrounds for use in wet weather. Where the buildings are already completed it would be worth an experiment to convert one or more of the flats to accommodate a play group.

By far the most serious evil to be eradicated, however, is damp. This curse afflicts hundreds of thousands of new houses and flats. The architects' and builders' excuses are not good enough. Why should they expect residents to live with their windows open throughout cold northern winters, or to keep heating in every room for twenty-four hours a day? The fact is that it is largely a matter of the design of the dwelling and the materials used. The excuses are invalidated by the fact that many designers and builders do manage to avoid damp, and yet keep within the cost yardstick.

There are a multitude of other building troubles: lifts which are seldom in working order; prestressed concrete which develops tiny cracks through which the rain seeps in, so that the whole of the exterior of a block of flats has to be resurfaced a year after completion; excessively creaking floors. And so on. In one month's council minutes of a single Town Council I found four items of repair work to blocks of new flats costing the sum of £180,000. I do not need to mention the collapse of the flats at Ronan Point, which required alterations to flats throughout the country costing more than £50 millions.

The National House Builders Registration Council does provide some security and compensation for private house purchasers against defective building. But local authorities are not covered by this scheme. They seldom prosecute firms which have involved them and their ratepayers in heavy loss. Why not? Reputable firms of architects and builders usually have large insurance policies against such damages.

To avoid some of these defects additional research would help. The national spending on housing research is infinitesimal – in contrast to the £330 millions a year for military research. The Government has announced a cut in its grant to the National Building Agency, which has done some excellent work on damp and other building problems. What is required is that more, not less, be devoted to research.

On council housing estates – particularly the older ones – more amenities to be provided. One naturally understands the priority given by councils to rehousing people. But houses by themselves are not enough. The time has now come not only to see that amenities are provided on new housing estates but also that they are added to old ones.

The success of the Scottish Special Housing Association, a publicly owned, non-profit making organisation, suggests that its example should be emulated south of the border. If such associations were set up in each of the six new metropolitan counties they could greatly help the local authorities in the conurbations, build homes at lower cost by large contracts and by saving the money which would have gone in profit to private firms, and carry out work in parts of the areas where the local Council was failing in its duty to build urgently needed houses.

Helping the private landlord's tenant

There is considerable dissatisfaction amongst private tenants, including those living in relatively good flats, with the way the 1968 Housing Act is working out. Its one solid achievement was to provide security of tenure to those in unfurnished lettings, providing, of course, they were not in rent arrears. Tenants of furnished dwellings have far less security. Except where the property is the landlord's home, they should be given the same protection against eviction as unfurnished tenants receive.

Instead of restoring reasonable rents after they had been decontrolled under the 1957 Housing Act, present legislation is being used to raise rents to an average of 2·6 times their previous controlled level. More landlords than tenants are now making applications to the rent fixing machinery. Of rents registered by rent officers in 1970, 75·8 per cent were increased compared with previous rents, only 17·5 per cent were reduced, and the remainder were unchanged. And certain companies owning large numbers of London flats are twisting the rules.

What has been worse is the disastrous part of the 1968 Housing Improvement Act, which took out of the existing rent control houses and flats in which the landlord installed a bathroom, hot water system and lavatory, or in which they already existed. Finally, the Housing Finance Act of 1972 takes the remaining $1\frac{1}{4}$ million tenants out of control.

One way to save private tenants about to lose their rent control is to offer them, at that moment of time, the opportunity of buying their houses from the landlords at a reasonable price. Local authorities should be encouraged to offer low-deposit or no-deposit mortgages at low interest rates to sitting tenants wishing to buy such houses. If the tenant declines the opportunity to purchase, the Council should be permitted to buy the dwellings at the same price. If, however, the landlord did not wish to take the house out of control and raise the rent in this way – and there are many houses where the landlord has not made use of his powers under the earlier legislation – then he would not be required to offer it for sale.

What would be a 'reasonable rent'? It should be clear that, as things are today, if rents of houses are sharply increased the market selling price of those houses will also rise steeply. I am indebted to Mr James Wellbeloved MP for a formula which would give the landlord more than he would get if the house were sold today with a controlled rent and a sitting tenant, but less than he would be able to charge following decontrol.

Some landlords complain that they wish they could be free of the burden of their properties. Here is a way they could be so and still obtain a fair return. They could then invest the sum realised in more lucrative undertakings. Not only would this lead to more improvements, but also to more repairs, being undertaken. The occupants, once they had become owner-occupiers, would see to this far better than their present landlords.

I have twice tried to introduce a Private Member's Bill along these lines – without success. However, this is not necessarily the end of the story.

More new towns

New towns and green belt cities are the ideal alternative to over-crowding in our old towns, and the forcing of families into multi-storey blocks of flats, which many of them strongly dislike. In new towns it is possible to start right from the beginning, with proper town planning, new homes, factories, schools, roads and amenities. The annual rate of building such new towns should be greatly accelerated. And so must be the number of jobs made available there.

Similar benefits can often be obtained by expanding existing towns, as is being done at Runcorn, Warrington and elsewhere. In this way the needs of the newcomers for jobs and entertainment can more easily be provided for during the early years of residence in their new homes.

There are critics who argue that land in Britain is so precious and is being encroached on so rapidly that we cannot afford to construct new towns in the countryside. They lack a sense of proportion. Take an aircraft flight from London to Manchester, a route which passes over the most thickly populated part of England. Even so, it will be quickly realised what a small part of the countryside is built up. Far better a green belt city than miles of ribbon building along busy roads. If there is a conflict of interest between millions of ill-housed city dwellers and a small number of farmers it seems fairly clear who should come first.

How to find the money

Why is it that West Germany, a country with an almost identical population and a similar economic system to ours, builds one and a half times as many houses a year as we do? There is no miracle involved. It is not that German building trade employees work any harder than ours. The explanation is that West Germany devotes one and a half times the proportion of her gross national product to housing compared with Britian.

Even in 1968, which was our record year for house building, we come near the bottom of the league table of industrialised nations in this respect. The share of national production devoted to house building in that year was:

France 6·7 per cent
Japan 6·5 „ „
Sweden 6·2 „ „
Germany 5·0 „ „
The USA 3·6 „ „
Britain 3·7 „ „

It is quite clear that if we are to end Britain's housing tragedy we will have to devote a greater proportion of the country's resources to doing so. More homes will need more money. Where is it to be found?

First, by an expansionist economic policy, with the 6 per cent per annum growth advocated by the TUC. Such a growth in production, of course, would provide more for housing and other social services even without raising the proportion of the national income devoted to them.

Second, an annual wealth tax on those with fortunes of over £50,000. It would hardly reduce those taxpayers to the supplementary benefit level. If, at the time such a tax was introduced, the Government indicated that it was going to spend more on helping the homeless, a wealth tax would be both just and popular. Although it was omitted from its election programme at the joint meeting of the national executive of the Labour Party and the Parliamentary leaders shortly before the last election, I hope it will feature in the next election manifesto.

While there is no space here to develop either of the above proposals, a little more attention should be given to a third one with huge potential. Though it is continually overlooked, it is staring us in the face.

When the Cabinet meets to discuss the allocation of resources, the Chancellor of the Exchequer, well briefed by his Treasury officials, opens with the national financial situation. He explains the limited funds available for social reform or, at times of crisis, why they must be cut. Then the Chancellor sits back. He has thrown the ball onto the field of play – or rather onto the Cabinet table. It is for the members to decide which players must be penalised.

One after the other, Ministers rush to defend their sphere of operations. The Secretary of State for the Department of Health and Social Security explains how, if promised reforms are to be brought into being, a higher allocation is required. The spokesman for the Department of the Environment intervenes to press the expensive road schemes which he maintains must be undertaken if traffic is not to be halted.

The raising of the school leaving age will require so many extra million pounds, the Secretary of State for Education and Science hastens to point out. Similar eloquent pleas are made by Ministers responsible for developing industry, agriculture and all the other departments – including housing. If they do *not* make such appeals they may be failing in their concern or their duty.

Of course, the score of Cabinet Ministers know that, if there had been a great leap forward in national output, they could all enjoy a larger slice of the cake. But the Chancellor's figures show only a minute rate of advance. Therefore something, or several things, will have to go. Where is the axe to fall?

There is only one sphere in which the Cabinet can cut without hurting ordinary working people – and that is military expenditure. Arms reduction would help – not hinder – the prospect for peace, by reducing international suspicion and tension. It might well encourage other nations to make even greater cut-backs. If the fantastic spending of £2,854 millions a year on arms could be reduced to the same proportion of our gross national product as that of other Western European NATO countries then most of the problems facing our country could be solved.

For, while we are at the bottom of the table as regards the share of the GNP devoted to housing, we are at the top of the table in Western Europe as regards the share going to 'Defence'. Only Portugal, pursuing its colonial war in Africa, devotes a higher proportion.

The following reply was made by Lord Balniel, Minister of State for Defence, on November 25, 1971:

On the latest available figures, Britain spent in 1970 5·7 per cent of her gross national product on defence, as compared with an average for NATO Europe of 4·2 per cent. If British defence spending were cut to 4·2 per cent of GNP there would be a saving of the order of £600 million.

He then gave the following details:

Percentage of GNP spent on defence – European members of NATO, 1970.

	1970% *of GNP*
Belgium	3·1
Denmark	2·8
France	4·7
Greece	5·7
Holland	3·9
Italy	3·0
Luxembourg	0·9
Norway	3·9
Portugal	7·0
Turkey	4·9
United Kingdom	5·7
West Germany	3·7
NATO Europe	4·2

So – even without quitting NATO – Britain could save £600 millions a year, just by coming down to the same percentage allocation as the average for other European NATO nations. If we reduced to the level of Italy it would save far more. France has declared its intention to reduce her arms spending to 3 per cent of the GNP by 1975. If we, sensibly, did the same, we should have £1,080 millions a year for other and better things. Housing would be one of the major beneficiaries.

With a far smaller sum than that added to existing housing resources we could start to build Jerusalem in England's green and pleasant land. It is for the people of Britain to decide whether they want arms expenditure to continue to grow or to be cut. If it is allowed to swell then we can say good-bye to the half million houses a year and most of the housing developments discussed in this book.

The choice is between bathrooms and bombers, between houses and H-bombs. If they were given the choice there is little doubt what most people would plump for. And it is for the people to decide. We live in a democracy. With all its limitations, if men and women in a democracy want something badly and determinedly enough they can get it.